Pause – A Spiritual Power

Pause – A Spiritual Power! What a concept... what a simple invitation... and what an effective reminder that it is possible to stop the insanity of "never enough," and the endless distractions of the mind. Rob Wykes has hit the PAUSE button in his own life, and through dozens of insightful vignettes has given us plenty to relate to in our own. He writes about the transformational soul-food offered by pilgrimage, by retreat, by any momentary gap lived with attention. Along the way he shares the words of great mystics and lovers of truth, from all traditions, inspiring his readers to take a deep, conscious breath. Ahhh, what then?
Regina Sara Ryan, retreat director and author of *Praying Dangerously* and *Igniting the Inner Life*

On BBC Radio 4, occasionally they have a slot called *Slow Radio*. The sounds vary greatly, but what they do is to invite us, just for a few moments, to disengage from the business of life – and be still.
Pause – A Spiritual Power invites us to do the same. This is not a religious book. Wykes, who comes from the Christian tradition, is not here interested in converting anyone to a particular religious belief or practice, but rather to the exploration of the spirit within.
Read this book slowly, take your time and let the wisdom, often disguised in an anecdote of daily living, seep deeply into your soul.
This is not a book of facts to be learned or techniques to be remembered and practiced. It is not rocket science, it is far more important than that. It is about you and me in the depths of our humanity and the spirit within.

I can heartily recommend this book to anyone wanting to discover a greater depth in life, and in themselves.

Chris Scott, retired psychologist, psychotherapist and priest, author of *The Jesus Myth*

In *Pause – A Spiritual Power*, Rob Wykes gives expression to an experience which most of us have had at least once, but which defies simple description: those moments when we come into sudden communion with God, when we are put in touch with the mystery – and joy – of our existence. Though these moments of respite from distraction and busyness – these "pauses" – are elusive, they are also, as Wykes shows, deeply important to a full-fledged spiritual life. Wykes proves an entertaining and accessible guide to how we might all learn to harness the power of pausing; where and how he's found these moments is both surprising and inspiring. His book has helped me tremendously in learning to seek, and to seize, pauses in my own life, and has swiftly become an invaluable addition to my spiritual bookshelf.

Macy Halford, author of *My Utmost: A Devotional Memoir*, and literary reviewer

Reading through the pages of *Pause – A Spiritual Power* by Rob Wykes, I found new insight into my old problem: how do I enter into my own spirituality? I had long since realized that religion is often about education and knowledge; church is mostly a social structure. They have their place, but ironically, are seldom about real spirituality. *Pause* brought me into an understanding of spirituality being a separate, unique place in life, one we "do" by not "doing" anything.

Pause is a friendly guide to accessing our spiritual selves. Through Rob Wykes's storytelling, sense of humor, and his own adventures – physical and spiritual – I found direction and possibility. Here is a map of what spirituality is and isn't, of the paths that are dead ends and those that lead to something transcendent. *Pause* is a book well worth reading.

Ken Petersen, author and publisher

Previous Title

It's Not About The Furniture
ISBN 978-1-78972-706-7

Pause – A Spiritual Power

Discovering the Entrance to Our Spirituality

Pause – A Spiritual Power

Discovering the Entrance to Our Spirituality

Rob Wykes

Winchester, UK
Washington, USA

JOHN HUNT PUBLISHING

First published by O-Books, 2023
O-Books is an imprint of John Hunt Publishing Ltd., 3 East St., Alresford,
Hampshire SO24 9EE, UK
office@jhpbooks.com
www.johnhuntpublishing.com
www.o-books.com

For distributor details and how to order please visit the 'Ordering' section on our website.

ISBN: 978 1 80341 336 5
978 1 80341 337 2 (ebook)
Library of Congress Control Number: 2022912470

A CIP catalogue record for this book is available from the British Library.

Design: Lapiz Digital Services

UK: Printed and bound by CPI Group (UK) Ltd, Croydon, CR0 4YY
Printed in North America by CPI GPS partners

The author of this book does not dispense medical advice or
prescribe the use of any technique as a form of treatment for
physical, emotional, or medical problems without the advice of a
physician, either directly or indirectly. The intent of the author
is only to offer information of a general nature to help you in
your quest for emotional and spiritual well-being. In the event
you use any of the information in this book for yourself, which is
your constitutional right, the author and the publisher assume no
responsibility for your actions.

We operate a distinctive and ethical publishing philosophy in
all areas of our business, from our global network of authors to
production and worldwide distribution.

Contents

At the early stages of writing *Pause*, kind friends, you know who you are, funded our living expenses whilst I completed this manuscript. To each of you, I dedicate this book.

Acknowledgements

Not because she is my wife but because without her love and endless patience in listening to the unfolding of my thoughts I could not have got here. – Thank you, Cheryl, let's have some fun.

I pay tribute to Ken Petersen for helping to pull together my thoughts, make sense of my ideas and hone my use of language. Working with Ken is like having a grocery bag full of raw ingredients and instead of following a recipe in a book the master chef sits at the table and instructs you on when and how and why each ingredient joins the pot. Ken helped make *Pause* a meal to savor.

Macy, Paul, Peter, Ben, Biju, Cheryl, and Ern – thank you for reading and at times pushing back on my thoughts. More than a sounding board you encouraged me to keep going.

There are friends and colleagues mentioned in this text without whom some of my stories would have been dull or nonexistent. Thank you for the memories we have built together.

Introduction

Thirty-eight years on from my first encounter with spirituality and religion, a friend asked if I really believed all that stuff. By *that stuff*, he was referring to a traditional paint-by-numbers religion, the kind that talks of spirituality in material terms. Being challenged to articulate what I believed in caused me to separate my personal spirituality from my tribe's portrayal of what is spiritual. What I had begun to understand about spirituality was quite different from anything I'd heard in my church.

It is a strange and exposing thing to unfold our inner thoughts in public, yet here I will. For many years I have read books on spirituality and made attempts to practice spiritual exercises. Much of my own personal spiritual journey has been in contrast to those around me. I was brought up in a home where God and spirituality had no place, and so when I first encountered religious life it was all new to me. I was like a sponge drawing in everything I saw and heard.

Spirituality, so I was led to believe, is expressed in actions. Being good and kind and not smoking or getting drunk seemed to be the marks of a spiritual person. So I tried to clean up my act, as it were, which made me a little judgmental of others. Then I found that knowing what we stood for in our religion and being able to articulate these things accurately to others was a sign of my spiritual progress. I became quite convinced the world was a black-and-white place, a world of those in and those outside the club. I honestly thought being spiritual was about believing and doing right things.

For too many years spirituality for me was intellectual and physical. It's not.

Spirituality is distinct from rational thought. Spirituality is not an activity of the mind, an act of thinking. I have come to recognize that to grasp this is hard but not impossible.

Likewise, spirituality is not about what we *do*. We tend to see religion as our spiritual life, and often we go to temples, mosques, or churches thinking we are being spiritual by being present or performing rituals. Yet religion tends to make the pursuit of spirituality into actions and ministries and programs.

But spirituality is not a doing thing or speaking thing. It is not meditating or contemplating. It's not prayer or preaching. These may bring us close to the doorway of spirituality, but in and of themselves they are not spirituality.

You may not, but I happen to believe God exists, and I identify as a practicing Christian. That doesn't mean I accept all Christian teaching or reject all other wisdom, religious or not. In this book I will express how spirituality is fundamentally about the spirit that is within us, how when we acknowledge the role of our spirit within we enter what I describe as a *pause*. I ask just one thing of you: whatever religious affiliation or philosophical perspective you hold, that you recognize you have a spirit. My hope is that as we journey through these chapters you will come to a place not of greater intellectual understanding, though that will be good, but to a place of communion and participation with the spirit within you.

For many years my friend Paul and I met once a week for what we called "Silent Prayers."

Before spirituality came to the fore of our friendship, Paul and I shared some mutual interest, along with others in our circle, in moaning about politics, prices, and people. But our friendship drove us deeper, and Paul and I decided to set off on a shared spiritual journey. We decided to share in this designated time of Silent Prayer.

Sitting in silence for prayers was for us a different way to meet and influence each other. Each Thursday at four in the afternoon we sat together behind the closed door to my office for thirty minutes. We didn't talk but remained in silence. At first it was hard to block out the background sounds that pierced the walls. My office was on the first floor of the busy community charity building where at the time I was the CEO. Directly underneath us was a cycle repair workshop – the ringing of hammers on metal and the noisy banter of the volunteers sounded loud and clear. To add to the cacophony were the furniture reuse teams shouting instructions as they loaded waiting delivery vehicles. A partition wall separated us from the finance office where our normally quiet and amazing administrator, Caroline, would occasionally burst out with a word in her native German – always entertaining.

I first met Paul after he retired from a career in marketing and sales. He joined the charity as a volunteer. In fact he joined a very specific group of enthusiasts bent on rescuing and restoring anything with two wheels. They were passionate about helping people lay hold of a cheap cycle.

Paul had long practiced meditation, much in the way you might think a Buddhist would. His education and the formation of his early encounter with spirituality had been delivered by monks. He has what I refer to as a rounded appreciation of reflective spirituality. Perhaps this came from his early years of experience in lighting a candle and watching the light flicker or hearing the nightly sound of compline being chanted. It was on my own spiritual journey that Paul helped me to see the value of making room in your day for intentionally holding a mirror to your soul. He would always say that we ask too many questions and that the questions we ask are invariably answered in silence.

You might question why we chose that particularly loud corner of a public building to attempt silent prayers. It may seem that it would have been easier had we found a quieter place to develop a new spiritual exercise. Yet learning spiritual reflection and meditation in a place filled with distractions seemed more realistic to me. I liked to know what's going on in my organization, so the noise was stimulating. In a strange way it comforted me. And in seeking silence I learnt quickly that the internal noise started to drown out the external, and that this is where a more refined and reflective spirituality began to emerge.

And so we sat in silence and in prayer. Eventually my body would become relaxed, not restless, and my mind would stop whirring or working things out.

Before my work took me elsewhere, Paul and I managed almost ten years of Thursdays sitting in silence. It was a starting place for a deeper understanding of what I will share with you as a call to moments of pause.

Along my journey, one I continue to travel, I have learned that we can move beyond concern for our body and our thoughts. I discovered that, occasionally, a place of access to the spirit within us opens up. Right there is where pause is found.

There are many ways in which we can find moments of pause. Pause is a familiar word we use without thinking. "Pause the TV whilst I'm on the phone," we shout to the kids. We pause for a comfort break after a meeting. In a crime novel we read, "He pauses before taking the shot." But in the context of this book, I use this word to describe a space between our normal rational approach to life and the spiritual world at the very edge of all we can imagine, a world just at the fingertips of our mortal grasp. The need for, access to, and gain from a mental or physical rest is obvious to many of us. What's more elusive is the realm of the spirit within us. Could there be access points or triggers we can encounter or use to deepen our moments of pause? This book seeks to open up that question and offer some reflection as we inch forward in our quest for a richer spirituality.

Along our journey, with all its talk and travel, its hustle and bustle, we can encounter moments when words cannot be found, when the walking is complete and where our will is for nothing beyond that moment. That moment is where the power of a pause opens our eyes to see what is always present, the spirit within us.

Many of the insights and experiences I share are personal, and my hope is that from them you may draw fuel for your own spiritual quest. Just such a quest has led me to what might be described as deep and rich encounters with my own being. From those with a belief in God we might hear a pause described as a place so personally intimate that it is where the kiss of God is most warmly felt. You will find your own way of experiencing this inner place.

I've never been comfortable with suggesting that my own pathway to spirituality is one of certainty for others. The very nature of our spiritual journey is that of individuality – it is just that – our journey. I have discovered over decades what I now describe as a pause, and this creates for me a sense of familiarity and confidence in how I express it. But to describe the pathway to a pause in the way, say, you would for making a cake would be to oversimplify how it is reached. I cannot give a cause-and-effect guarantee. Many of us have grown beyond the instructional, even fashionable, directives of what constitutes spirituality. This is because spirituality is in large part a mystery. I cannot say, "If you breathe this way and sit that way you will experience a moment of pause," because spirituality is much more subtle and personal than that.

What I place before you is not certainty, but simply the road which I travel, a road which I have found to bear signs of wisdom and hints of possibility. It is a road I invite you to walk with me now.

My friend Paul – like many who seek spirituality, God, or a deeper understanding – never aligned himself with any particular religious affiliation. He was not tribal, and this enhanced our conversation and prayer time. Our only rule was *observe silence*.

You may come to realize that I have beliefs in a number of areas, but please know I don't ask or need you to come to them in the same way. To bend an ancient Jewish text, "We are *individually* and wonderfully made." We are not all the same, and in that is the most wonderful bit. Like an exotic fruit, the spirit within is not hanging from one specific tree that we all harvest from in the same way.

I don't need you to believe what I believe. But I have tasted something with my spiritual taste buds – pause – and my desire is that you too will taste and see that it is beyond the conventions of belief and religion.

Over the years I have identified a moment of pause as having a central definition: the moment our body, mind, and spirit coalesce in an unmeasurable, unrestricted moment. At just such points of experience our being has no conscious awareness of the need to be anyone or anywhere else in that given moment. Our intellectual capacity is vital, our body is an amazing structure, yet I want to show how much richer life is when we see we are more than our thoughts and more than our physical bodies.

I ask that you might walk with me to seek out moments of pause in the ordinary and chaotic, and in the general run of life both planned and impromptu, where we discover the precious reality of our whole being at rest and in concert.

Pause

Part One

What It Is, What It Isn't, and Why We Need It

"*Some* reduce themselves to a life lived within the limits of their five senses."[1]
But it doesn't have to be so.

Chapter 1

The Problem and Promise of Pause

Imagine spending three hours hiking to the brow of a hill which gives way to a breathtaking view. From such views we instinctively sense something – our spirit draws life from creation. Still and sitting, we begin to take it all in as we pour hot coffee from the thermos flask. These are brief but wonderful moments.

A small grey patch of cloud bleeds into the clear sky, stealing the moment. It threatens to rain on us, an unwelcome soaking. Now, all we can think of is the long precarious walk downhill to the car. At first we consider sticking it out, so we dismiss the idea of turning back. But that thought is short-lived as we remember that we hadn't packed for bad weather. The moment has gone! The cloud is now filling our hearts, not just the sky. We eat with haste and drink the coffee before it has cooled, and set off downhill.

Two damp and drizzly hours later, feeling hot and sticky, we are sitting steaming up the windows in the car. Holding the key in the ignition, I try to retain the brief but extraordinary sense of being alive that I had at the hilltop where momentarily our journey had been rewarded with a spiritual connection to the beauty before me.

The moment is gone. But while the rain may have dampened my mood, the breathtaking view would have delighted my spirit. It was a moment of spiritual pause, well worth the climb and the journey.

During my first ten years of growing and developing a small local charity helping people with practical support, we had many consecutive hilltop moments, successes if you will. It was a time when we bounced from one new project to the next without catching breath. We were always so propelled towards the next exciting thing, it was a challenge to stop and enjoy the achievements along the way. At the launch event of a cycle repair shop for young people, we resented having to stop our work for a dignitary visit and a photo opportunity. Our feeling was this was time we could have spent more productively. Standing and smiling for the camera in a new workshop was time we could have spent fixing bikes or teaching skills. It was never natural or comfortable for me to pause the operational activity to savor or celebrate a milestone.

There are clearly times when we arrive at a place that feels naturally ripe for a break, an opportunity to enjoy what has been gained or reached. Yet many of us are wired to press on. In doing so we miss the promise of a memorable moment.

In Scotland, mountains over 3,000 feet are called a *Munro*. To climb and reach the top means you have "bagged a Munro." I once met a Munro-bagger who was on target to ascend all 282. He described reaching the top, ticking that particular Munro off his list and then continuing on. Sometimes he didn't even stop. It seemed such a waste to me that he rarely stopped to enjoy the moments at the top.

This is how some of us do life. We barely break our stride even when standing before us there is a wonderful invitation to stop and allow our spirit to draw life in. In our thirst for the next summit in life we can, at times, pass over the encounter with the spiritual.

Every next task or project seems exciting, and pausing to simply "be" in a moment seems like wasted time. We skip over what may seem an empty space. A space which is in fact a break in the line of doings which make up only a part of our whole being. The space between these words I write matters, and you will agree it helps to make sense of the words on either side. At times in life we see those in-between spaces as empty or unproductive because there are other things on our list to be doing. I want to suggest that those moments sitting on the hilltop, stopping the operational activity, or switching off the engine, are indeed productive. They are moments fertile for spirituality, beauty, and mystery.

Have you ever noticed the almost imperceptible still moment when we breathe out? Having exhaled, we don't immediately draw breath but delay the return pull. There is a moment that we never quite take note of; a moment when we are neither breathing nor not breathing. Right there in that space our need for air is suspended – we pause from the very thing we presume to bring us life, yet we continue to live. So we can let go, albeit briefly. and maybe in that space find life that is more than the air we breathe.

There are times when we place an urgency or importance, maybe unaware and without intention, on the next thing to do. We can find living in the future easier than the present because it has the feel of forward movement. This can seem a natural pull in life – we are as it were leaning forward as though reaching into the future. The lights turn green and before we clear the junction we have shifted to second gear and without thought proceeded up through the gears, seamlessly and without identifiable pause. Doing life this way we can so often forget, even fail to savor and enjoy, the spaces or passing moments of stillness which are stolen by our living in the next thing to do. Like good food, the second you swallow, the tasting is over, and the temptation is to load up with the next fork-full.

As natural and perhaps exciting as living in the future is, living in the past has its attraction too – we sense it to be a familiar place. Time we spend thinking and feeling our way through yesterday's journey can bring with it a measure of warm nostalgia, a better place than the present moment. Surely I'm not alone in taking comfort in the memory of when I ran the distance of a half marathon. I can project in my mind an image of being back out there, swift as gazelle, yet I imagine my past self from within my unfit-and-struggling-to-walk-fast present self. I really liked the *me* back there!

You see, the past and the future are places we can identify with, places we may find a perceived better version of ourselves. To pause is only possible in the present, fully in the self we really are. To pause is to be utterly whole and utterly present in a given moment – at the point of transition, if you will – between present and future events, between actions, between thoughts. A pause can be as subtle as the space between breaths or as profound as an hour of meditation. A pause cannot take place without unity of body, mind, and the spirit within us. To pause is about getting to a point at which we are whole.

We have to acknowledge that the concept I am putting forward of a pause, a spirituality if you will, is abstract and hard to express. Yet I believe that the spirituality found in a pause is as real and as identifiable as any sense of reality we encounter in the material world, just not measured or expressed so easily. So, to pause is a present experience. We may, like all experiences, look back at a moment of pause and hope to encounter more in the future – they too are part of our past and future – but the richness and power of a pause is very much a *present* experience.

The idea of being present in the present is not a new concept and is one well documented. Psychology books line the shelves of bookstores and wellness centers where meditation, relaxation, and contemplation are the zeitgeist – the thing of the day. Some of these techniques are of great benefit. An old friend of mine, Theo, practiced psychotherapy and spoke often of helping to guide a patient towards being present in the present. Some people can struggle to identify with the present moment because of a difficult or tragic past experience. In therapy these people are working to live in a present reality, not their past scars. I have seen real positive change in people who have achieved this change in their thinking. However, this is not what I mean by a pause being a present moment, a sort of moment of presence of mind. Theo was taking a psychological approach, which is much about rationalized thinking, knowing, and controlling thoughts in the present. But a pause is not a moment we contrive or conjure up, not a controlled track of thought we follow. It is more an unplanned convergence of the body, mind, and spirit within us. We don't think or manipulate our way into a pause. We arrive at it and enter.

Speaking on the subject of "becoming stillness," Richard Rohr, the Trappist monk, mentioned the writings of Eckhart Tolle. Rohr had written to Tolle pointing out that in his book *The Power of Now* Tolle is, "taking the great Christian tradition that we called the sacrament of the present moment or the grace of the present moment and is really just speaking it to us in modern terms." There is of course nothing wrong with restating or rephrasing what many of the mystics of the third and fourth century – who built the spiritual traditions Rohr speaks of – came to understand as present experience.

I believe they discovered that the journey to spiritual presence is a gift granted not a gain earned. This is why Rohr uses the words "sacrament" and "grace." The present is not a place entered by mindfulness or techniques designed to usher us through a door which is simply waiting for our mind to turn the key. We cannot *think* our way into the present, for it is between, not of, our thoughts.

On this pathway many people discover a rich space, which I believe is an in-between moment where they cease to bargain with their thoughts and their God. That space is what I identify as a pause, a present moment when the spirit within us breathes. In that space of pause, we know intuitively that life is more than the material or mental world.

Our lives are filled with moments of possibility: "Soft places of our life's landscape, in which it seems that eternity presses close upon time,"[2] says Mark Barrett. He is exploring the experience of Morning Prayer when the rising of the sun creates moments of openness or transition from the night to the day, a point where we might discover a pause.

To even begin to discover these in-between moments, or the space we may call the present, is not easy for some people, especially in the Western world. Here we have created an approach to life which seems to reduce our quiet time. We have limited the available time where we might discover the power of our true spirituality. The development of a social structure that soaks up our waking hours with well-engineered stress has greatly impacted us.

Our patterns of work and pressure to conform and perform have removed our physical and mental downtime. Simply existing has become complex. Thirty years ago we would have a phone installed in the house and paid a monthly bill. There would be few problems. We might go a year or two with no reason to contact the phone company. Now we might have more than one phone, each of which needs the contract renewed, the phone upgraded, and the data reviewed every year. This same pattern of complex and stressful interactions is replicated in every part of living. It squeezes us into a place of seeing every second and resource as in need of measuring and protecting.

But fear not because the stress engineers have created parallel industries that churn out new and creative de-stress lifestyle remedies. The phone app offers 10% off at a relaxing spa. The loyalty points built up from shopping at Jimmy's Store mean you can now go to a meditation class! The net result for many of us feels like being inside a wheel round which we run continuously, in constant stress. Even with promises of de-stress, we never stop to experience those moments in-between where a pause may be found.

Occasionally when we think there is room to break free, the excitement is stifled by another spin round the wheel! Like the

Hotel California in the Eagles song: "You can check-out any time you like but you just can't leave." In the year 2000 my friend bought me a personal time management system – a glorified diary! Along with millions of others, I started in January. By mid-February it was taking an hour a day to fill out workflow charts, pre-meeting resource audits, and advance weekly/ monthly and yearly planners.

The sales pitch for the latest time management life coaching app assures us we will be freed up to do the things we just have no time for now. What we end up with are seamless links to the next things to do. I share this because for some of us the idea of there being a still moment in the present, a transition point where everything may stop, can seem unimaginable.

We are right to identify the need to discover space between the events of life. Our instinct though is to have an app to help us have a plan to put breaks in those events of life. This of course becomes another event: we say that during 13:00 till 13:30 we will sit quietly and switch on the spontaneous spirituality tap. Really? I have known times when I have created the space in my own schedule for spirituality time. If only it were that easy! We can force time in our schedules for a pause, but we cannot switch it on or off. A moment of pause *happens* in the spaces in-between – it cannot be manufactured as a planned event. We need room in our lifestyle into which moments of pause can enter, but we cannot make pause happen.

I have come to accept that it takes more than a line in a book, an app on the phone, or the gift of a diary to move us towards the kind of change that stays. How often from the unplanned incidents of life have we encountered something that brought lasting change to us or opened our eyes to new possibilities? A routine doctor's checkup reveals high cholesterol, and our response is an action we have always known would bring a benefit to our body – less fat and sugar. Likewise, learning to identify and value the space in-between can come to us on the back of a revelation, perhaps through a difficult time or tragedy that delivers a dire prognosis – that we are spiritually broken and need to change our lives to make space for spiritual healing.

Historical, political, and personal events that we neither foresee nor control can move us in directions we would not have previously considered and prompt us to attend to our spiritual selves. Events such as entering a recession, going through a war, or a death in the family can change our fixed positions. Certainly a pandemic resets our priorities. My grandparents' generation lived through the 1918 Spanish flu pandemic and it shifted the way they valued time together. My parents' generation survived the Second World War, and the lesson of food rationing tweaked their approach to nutrition. My children have some memory of the confusion over evidence for the two Gulf Wars, and are much less willing than my parents to sign off on military campaigns. My grandchildren will one day explain to their children what COVID-19 meant.

These are all major transition points with a before and after. Doors through which we travel and transform.

All of these transition points are opportunities for us to be open to pause. A pause can be experienced in the midst of life-change, when we begin to allow our body and mind to adjust, to accommodate the spirit within us. These are specific points in time when we may physically and mentally cease our journey, when the world seems to stop. It is in these gaps in the events of our lives where all that we are and all that we need are revealed in a present moment. Our body and mind have union with the spirit within us and we are complete. That is the point at which we pause.

In our desire for such moments we may introduce into our lives patterns of behavior which seek to create moments in-between where we hope to touch the realm of spirituality. For some of us the ancient spiritual practices such as meditation, prayer, and contemplation become ways to add into our daily life opportunities for us to get in touch with the spirit within.

Finding others with a similar set of spiritual desires can be helpful too.

Having known in-between moments, as I refer to them, we can begin to navigate what is and is not a pathway to pause for ourselves. For many of us there is a discovery that pause comes to us as we allow it to form a transcendent experience. It is as though we are naked of all flesh and thought – breathlessly encountering who we are beyond whatever constrains us.

For many of us with a faith this is the point of "divine connection," when the spirit within, not our emotions or intellect, bonds with our God. Yet as I have said, to pause in the way I have described is not an act of our will but a point at which our mind, body, and the spirit within enter into concert. It is a connection with ourselves first and foremost, difficult to predict, yet I believe unmistakable when in process and after.

For the best part of three decades my wife and I worked in a small town helping to create a vision of a better existence for some of society's poorest and most broken people. There were challenges, stress, and the odd moment of wanting to run away! In learning the nuance of finding the space between the exhale and inhale in our lives, we discovered that it was not about running away, letting go, or spending time trying to reconcile the contradictions in life. It was about creating a space between those contradictions, a time-out, a pause.

I enjoy reading John Grisham novels, many of which are centered around the courtroom. To break the drama and create a space at a point when everyone is too tired to follow the evidence, the judge says, "We'll adjourn until tomorrow." Tomorrow the crime will still exist and the evidence will need examining, but for now there is a space between those events. A pause is very like this, revealed in-between the processes of life, the breakpoints in which we find room to simply be.

I like a good restorative holiday (vacation), time away from work and a cultural change with food I normally would not eat. A pause may well happen whilst on holiday, but it is not the actual holiday, though refreshing it may be. Similarly the stimulation of a seminar, a well-led retreat or teaching session can be invigorating and provide time out – yet I would not describe the sessions as a pause. Each of these things has a strong element of intentional activity and mental stimulation. We might go on that quiet holiday to read a book and sit in the sun, yet we are intentionally relaxing, hoping to return rested or energized. This is different from a pause. A pause is about intentionally not doing anything. It is without a plan for future experience. A moment of pause happens when we enter a space we have not engineered ourselves to be in, however much we might hope for such an encounter.

From a holiday we may return physically rested or mentally uncluttered. We attend a seminar or teaching to bring change because by their nature we take challenges and questions along with us in hope of a solution and wise insight. We return with the said better feeling or clearer direction. Yet from a pause we return, not fitter or wiser, but changed by an experience of unquestioning wholeness. I want to emphasize the point that a pause is at its heart not about redress for the past or resources for the future – it is a self-contained beautiful transcendent moment of pure spiritual reality.

Matters of the body and mind are easy to grasp for us – they are tangible and relatable. The challenge comes in grasping the abstract notion of the spirit within us. I know this is something that doesn't sit well in a world of making and building and conquering and growing. We want clear and unambiguous directions. But there is no user manual for finding and experiencing pause. Our only instruction is to be open to it when it happens.

The stories and illustrations in this book are a serious meander through the various ways I saw moments of pause take place and how they impacted the way I now approach life. Whilst I will go back many years with my reflections, my real journey began whilst I took a sabbatical in 2018. It was then I had an extended time to look into my own heart and interrogate my own spirituality. I read of the lives of many who undertook to discover their essential person or true self as some describe it. I came away convinced that we find, almost always by chance, an entrance to a pause when aware of or seeking connection with the spirit within us. Yes, we must be open and searching, create space and place in our lives where our body, mind, and the spirit within us can come together without conflict or competing. That is why we can't be in the past or future, leaving or arriving.

Like many others who discover a richer spirituality, I seem to retain in my busy life what friends and colleagues describe as a constant smile. A smile in a life filled with a beautiful mountaintop quickly covered in rain, loving people interspersed with unkindness, hopes fulfilled and dashed. The smile is not about being happy but in knowing that life in the fullest and most complete sense is more than what we do or think. Christians often speak of us being accepted just as we are, that God is not looking for us to do more but simply to chat with us. I like that. I like that we are deeper than what we do.

Many years ago, one sunny afternoon on our village green we held a tug-o-war match. Lines of the heaviest people from the local pub and our church held the long rope. Red ribbons for markers were tied round the middle of the rope and then others a meter or so either side. The umpire called for the tension to be held. The rope squeaked under the strain as the umpire's voice shouted in a drawn-out way, "Steady, steady!"

Sometimes a tug can seem to take ages because the teams are so well matched. On this occasion the red ribbons hardly moved as the villagers were screaming, "Pull, pull...!" Right there in the middle of that rope was a pause in the tension, nothing moved forward or back, and to let go would mean the other team would crumble in a pile.

I recall this moment often because life is so like that. We are committed, and one way or another that ribbon will move, but in that space between victory and defeat, success and failure, forward or back is where we can capture a pause. For subtle and lasting seconds an aspect of our being seems separated, apart, or removed from the tightness of life's tense moments.

On the field that day it was not so much a physical pause, though muscles continued to strain, but for a brief moment everything stopped, and I took in the surroundings. I for a moment forgot the strain. It was as though time was suspended. Moments later we were all on the floor covered in mud, winners! (I suspect the church team won not because we prayed beforehand or had God's favor on us but because our opponents had prepared in the pub by drinking for a couple of hours before the contest!)

Spotting the moment of pause in this physical world is, as one ancient writer put it, grasping hold of something which is elemental to life yet cannot be experienced by the physical senses. I suspect this is because when we enter a pause we have encountered the realm of the spirit within us. While we have no choice but to interpret, acknowledge, and even express a pause in terms of emotions, feelings or language yet it holds a place in our being which is beyond the reach of these things.

People, since the dawn of time, have been as busy and distracted as we are today. Like them we stop at the point of transition, between the exhaled and inhaled – for if anywhere it is there we will come across an entrance to the spirit within us and a moment of pause. These are those inexplicable seemingly unreal realities that each of us alone can pinpoint, and they appear as frozen time filled with otherworldliness – moments void of the cares of this world yet carrying a presence more present than conscious awareness itself.

If not spoken out loud, then our mind all too often fills the space separating life's events with, "What's next"! However important, tense, unavoidable, exciting, or pleasurable the next thing on our list to do is, imagine experiencing an in-between moment.

Why not listen to your breath and capture the pause at the bottom of the next exhale?

Pause

Chapter 2

Pausing without Thinking

Cyril was a faithful and passionate train driver. "Old school" was the way the younger railway staff at the station would describe him. A fireman on the famous Flying Scotsman, he had shovelled hundreds of tons of coal. That back-breaking work turned water to steam which powered the iron horse along its steel rails. Such unhealthy labor has all but disappeared from the modern Western workforce. He belonged to an industrial past which filled your lungs with smoke and coal dust and brought your end closer to your beginning.

The sitting room where he had rested each day after work for more than forty years was coated wall to wall in railway memorabilia. Cyril's wife, Betty, and their daughter and son sat motionless, faces revealing the pain and confusion of loss. Tears were flowing, and their moist eyes appeared to be a welcome release to their sorrowful hearts. The one constant in their lives was no longer present: Cyril had died peacefully in the hospice with his family by his side. As we planned his memorial service, Betty told me, "He should be laid to rest at the place he loved the most and spent much of his working life – on platform 5." A great idea, I thought, but as a mere chaplain I knew it was a wish for something not in my power to grant. Yet it did happen: Betty got her wish and we set about planning a service on the station platform.

The story of my encounter with this small family illustrates that in the briefest of moments, when the unexpected might happen, we don't have to rush to our intellect for answers. It is not uncommon to find ourselves in a place where our planning and preparation encounter an unanticipated situation. I want us to think in this chapter about how the power of a pause is not found in our thoughts nor even in our prayers but in the acknowledged presence of the spirit within us. We shall see how our natural and understandable default position in particular situations is to fumble about in the mind for words. Worse, we sometimes fill the void with nervous incoherent waffle. Yet the more we become tuned in to the spirit within, the more our lives find increasing familiarity and ease of access to moments of pause.

It took several attempts to negotiate, but two weeks after his death, we assembled at the station top and walked the cremated remains of Cyril down to the end of platform 5. At this time in my life I was the Railway Chaplain for the North West of England and Wales, covering all railway installations from Preston to Stoke-on-Trent and out to Holyhead in North Wales. This involved hundreds of hours of visiting the sick and bereaved. Conducting funerals was part of the role. Nervously, I held the urn bearing Cyril's ashes.

Strict health and safety protocols were in place as the mourners and I stood near a quiet part of the trackside. The railway company had been very helpful but the one accommodation they could not make was to stop the trains flowing through the middle of the station on what is known as the fast line. It was a poignant moment charged with expectation on the part of the mourners and some measure of anxiety on my own part.

Tilting the urn towards the rails on which Cyril had travelled many times I began to read the words for the internment of ashes drawn from the Genesis narrative in the first book of the Bible, "ashes to ashes," when I became aware of a rumbling sound. The eyes of those gathered around were no longer entirely fixed on me. We heard the unmistakable sound of steel wheels on steel track and felt a gust of air. The Manchester-bound express train passed through the station at speed. Although it was a good distance away, its length and speed stirred the air and pushed it across the station in our direction.

The next words to leave my mouth as I continued to pour the remains of Cyril onto the track now seemed most appropriate: "Dust to dust," and as I spoke those words we were being lightly coated with the remains of Cyril.

This was about as tense as it gets. All movement stopped. The assembled mourners looked at me as I held the now empty urn.

It was whilst coated in Cyril and in similar subsequent situations that I came to recognize the possibility of a simple few seconds of pause. It is as though a void opens up into which the onlookers are expecting, in this case from me, some kind of wisdom or direction to be poured. Yet I find in these moments I am better served by not grappling to meet their expectations.

Often when in a crisis situation people of faith offer up short prayers, or a plea sent skyward, if you will – brief thoughts populated with the words "help" and "please." "Arrow prayers," some may call them. Others might pray in this way when the thing to do next is unclear, yet there remains a strong sense that immediate action is needed. If you are a person of prayer, then you will know there is a comfort, even a sense of communion with the God you serve as you converse with that God. It's a bit like a child asking a parent, "What do you think I should do?" As I have stated, to pause is not an action of the mind but a resting in the spirit within us. To pray in awkward situations, however helpful or short, is still to enter a dialogue to form ideas or articulate a fear or frustration, albeit a dialogue taking place in the mind. To pray is to talk and to listen as we strain to hear a response by remaining alert mentally.

Ultimately praying is at its very core about an exchange, a transaction in which we seek an audience with our God. I have long understood that God exists to us in spiritual form, and so an audience with our God is a spiritual encounter not an intellectual one. I wonder then, how much of our prayers find their birth, life, and death taking place entirely within the mind, never making it to a spiritual level? By this, I mean to respectfully question how much of our praying dialogue is an internal mental conversation as opposed to a spiritual encounter with our God.

There is a vast difference between saying prayers and praying. This is not a new thought, many great spiritual leaders such as Gandhi, Mother Teresa, Saint Francis of Assisi, among others, recognized the need to go beyond words when they prayed. There is a well-used, perhaps apocryphal, story of a deeply spiritual monk. He is asked how long he prays each day. He replies, "Thirty to forty minutes." The questioner is taken aback and asks why such a short time. "Oh that's because it takes me all day to empty my mind of all the chatter and give room for my heart to rise." In the Psalms we find David a broken king praying for the creation of a pure heart and the renewing or restoring of his spirit within him. This all tells us that there is a profound part of us, the spirit within, which is separate from our thoughts. It is the seat of our spirituality. Like David of old and every other pursuer of spirituality, we use all the language at our disposal to articulate what is beyond our words as we grapple with the mystery of our spiritual being, communicating with a spiritual God.

Prayer, of course, does not have to be complex in thought and it could be argued that praying is a way into a period of spirituality. This is not unlike the track down which we might travel toward meditation or indeed the result of a verse or poem upon which we have spent time contemplating. The object of much meditation is to come to a place where our mind is less cluttered or clinging to information. Yet meditation, or mindfulness, requires a sort of warm-up process. A Buddhist may use a mantra or chant to journey toward clearing the mind. A Christian may meditate using the Jesus Prayer, in which he repeats over and over again, "Lord Jesus Christ, Son of God, have mercy on me, a sinner." Helpful as these refrains are, it seems to me that the repeated words are a mental exercise, a function of the brain, if you will. Still, I believe these exercises may result in a period when our body, mind, and the spirit within us find unity of being – that is, we become without need of thought. We pause. So, to meditate is at least to begin with a dialogue as though we talk our way into a place of *being apart from our thoughts*.

In his book *Breathing, I Pray*, Ivan Mann writes of hearing an Orthodox sister who frequently said, "The Jesus Prayer unfolds itself in the soul." Mann goes on to explain how years after he stopped praying the Jesus Prayer, he began to notice it was still there inside him. He writes, "I stopped praying the prayer, and it started praying in me."[3] I wonder if by this he had found that the spirit within us, not the mind, is at work beyond our conscious awareness.

For many years I could not recognize a distinction between meditation and contemplation. They are often used interchangeably. In the situation I found myself in at the memorial of Cyril, there was clearly no time to start the trip towards a meditation: people were watching and waiting for a response from me in the circumstance of Cyril's ashes becoming cloud around us.

When we find ourselves with a problem or invitation to fill a space with wisdom, our natural instinct is to hone in on the core of the situation – contemplate the options. I believe there is a point at which we find a pause in the space between our contemplations and meditations. I see meditation as being a reduction, as far as possible, of our thoughts; hence a short repeated line like the Jesus Prayer. To contemplate is to mull over something; it doesn't have to be spiritual, and it just requires our focused attention whilst we circle a subject in our mind.

We could look at it in these terms: that the words of our mantra are to push thoughts out of our mind, but many other words become conscious thinking, ideas that actually distract us from our spiritual reality. Like fluff gathering on our clothes in the tumble dryer, our thoughts gather more thoughts.

A challenge of my proposition about pause is that we are here thinking about what it means to be in a place of not thinking. It seems an impossibility, unachievable and to some a ridiculous proposition. It is in a way a matter of mental wrestling with the deeper sense of who we are as humans and yet finding a break in the mental wrestling.

It is reasonable to take the view that my idea of pause might be a philosophical muse with no foundation. That to speak of the spirit within can be too abstract an idea if there is no experience of spiritual reality for the one considering the proposition. We begin with thinking about pause as an idea but for the reality of it to take hold we move beyond thinking.

I remember as a teenager being dared by some mates to enter a dark abandoned factory unit. The rumor was the ghost of the last owner worked the machines at night which in the day lay rusting. You guessed it, the dare only worked if I went in at night. I spent all day thinking about what I might find, who I might meet and what might happen to me. My mates egged me on and eventually I stopped trying to rationalize it and climbed in through the window. I found the machines still motionless and no ghost. In fact I remember I quite enjoyed knowing I had been where the others hadn't. I joined a small group of local lads who ventured into the unknown.

In terms of pause, I long not to allow the challenge of intellectually explaining what might be behind the spiritual door to be the thing which keeps that door closed for me. This happens because we are excluding a part of our being which makes us whole. To discover moments of pause is not to increase knowledge or expand the thought world but to enter a different realm of our existence.

So to pause is not to pray nor to contemplate nor to meditate. As worthwhile as these are and as aspects of spiritual development most necessary, still they are primarily a function of our thoughts. They may lead us to moments of pause, but they are not pause, not purely engaging our spiritual selves.

One of the railway staff on duty the day we scattered Cyril's ashes was Mike, a man I had come to know well. He was one of those characters that had a phrase for everything. One of his well-known phrases, spoken to his young recruits in customer services, was, "Engage your brain before opening your mouth." He would mime zipping his mouth shut and buttoning it up, like a children's entertainer using lots of gestures to get his point over.

So inclined are we to this reaction of immediately speaking that we do need to be reminded to think first in many situations. Yet I want to go further back than zipping my lips and engaging my brain. To pause in the context of my experience at Cyril's memorial was not about scratching around to find the right words – engaging the brain – it was about avoiding that natural inclination of thinking by engaging with the spirit within.

There are circumstances in life when the audience before us is looking to us to fill a void and we are programmed, encouraged and, even taught to engage the brain by thinking. Nothing wrong with that but pause is about recognizing that approach is not the only one. There are unexpected situations forced upon us with dramatic tension, a tension which connects to our mental and emotional responses which threaten to dominate and mold our response. In the situation I described at the trackside when I was a serving Railway Chaplain everyone was looking at me. This is perfectly normal.

I believe it possible that our thought world can park up giving room for the spirit within us to breathe.

So, what did happen that day at the station on platform 5?

I didn't pray. I didn't start the process of moving into meditation, I didn't scurry about in my mind for words or prattle on with incoherent waffle. I found, because I knew from experience, an opening to the spirit within me. Only a matter of seconds passed, but it was much longer for me in spiritual time. Our spirituality is neither governed by the material world nor the fears of our intellectual world, and to know this is to become influenced less by our thoughts and more by the spirit within us.

My own thoughts were parked as I entered a moment of pause. As I returned with little conscious thought or restraint from my mind, I looked into the eyes of everyone gathered and felt their mourning and pain. In hindsight I would say their faces held a desperate desire to be released into respectful laughter.

As the sound of the speeding Manchester express left our ears and Cyril's ashes rested on the mourners I held their gaze and simply said, "Cyril brought you down here today so you could feel the thrill he had at the start of his working life on this platform. The power of a train rushing by, the texture of soot and ash from the boiler on you, and the mystery of a thousand journeys to who knows where."

Smiles and quiet laughter released into the air, filling the platform with memories of an old train driver – Cyril.

That particular situation only happened to me once, unforgettable but not repeated. Yet we see the scenario played out all the time in life and work.

Some years later I was invited to speak at Portcullis House, part of the Houses of Parliament, on the subject of community regeneration. The speaker before me had the most dreadfully slow PowerPoint presentation. Rather than sentences or words, individual letters crept across the screen like slugs. He lost his audience in the first sentence and his eyes told us he knew it. I watched as his time ran out and his panicking mind grappled for words. What to cut out, what to leave in. Then I saw him look out the window with what to most appeared an empty gaze; I had hoped for a pause for him.

There are times when we find ourselves at the heart of a crisis from which our logic seems incapable of rescuing us. I believe these to be opportunities fit for the spirit within us to be both our refuge and rescuer. The challenge of this book is to recognize the relevance of the spirit within not just in the quiet with a candle but the cut and thrust of life.

Chatting over coffee with that speaker who fumbled and froze along with his dreadful presentation he talked of his emotions gripping him and his mind feeling fast and frozen at the same time – meltdown is a good description. This was a space into which a pause would have fitted perfectly, but his thought world would not allow the spirit within room to breathe.

I have discovered that there are occasions when despite the preparation, prayer and practice runs put in to a point of engagement with others, something unpredictable can put a spanner in the works. There are unplanned situations, some with high tension, which can slip in creating momentary crises.

Included in the arsenal of possible responses to circumstances such as those described in this chapter is to move away from the dominance of a belief that all the answers we need are an exercise of our mind. In living a life of growing familiarity with the spirit within we can cultivate a route to pause. I believe praying, contemplating, and meditating lend more naturally to our disposition to think through life than to pause. That is until pause becomes one of our accepted and familiar aspects of life. Then in moments of crises with no notice we will find we have a well-worn and familiar pathway to a momentary pause.

Pause

Chapter 3

When Pause Is What You Need Most

I lay on the bed with the room spinning. I felt confused, sad, and angry with God and the world.

Earlier that day I had walked around the sites of Auschwitz and Birkenau, confronted by the terror of inhumanity and discovering the immense depth by which a soul can ache for others. Yet the words of a camp survivor, Irving Roth, inscribed in a stone near the gate, had begun to settle in my mind: "I decided that my quarrel was not with God, but with man."

His words challenged the simmering rage lurking within me. I have long suspected that we blame God for terrible things because the alternative is to see part of ourselves capable of enacting those terrible things. Later that evening, by God's good grace, I found myself listening to music composed by Chopin, a man in touch with the inner workings of our sometimes sensitive heart.

The day had begun well, with my driver and guide collecting me on time. This was important because I can get anxious when I'm not in control. Already I was nervous at what I might see and feel in going to Auschwitz. I was part of a small party, strangers to each other, as we headed towards one of Poland's most visited sights. Auschwitz was not too far from our starting place of Krakow but far enough to let the mind prepare for what would no doubt be cause for reflection, if not an adjustment of my world view.

I was visiting one of the world's most renowned monuments to human failure. I expected my encounter to hold emotional sadness and challenge my sense of justice. What I would be seeing would mess with my head and my heart. That much I knew. But as I moved through this experience, I discovered something which went beyond what we might call the emotional or mental encounter. A doorway opened to the story of one man in particular, which resonated with the spirit within me.

We speak of a pause as an in-between moment, the moment before we refill our lungs with fresh life, having just emptied them of stale air. Such moments can also be that space between encountering the story of a victim and discovering his survival, the time between vague information and specific knowledge.

Such was the horror and so powerful the emotions evoked by the tour, that I found myself beginning to shut things out. Voices of the guides became muffled, competing for bandwidth in the processor of my brain. I came away thinking it might have been better to make several short visits, as the volume of information was just too great a flood of obvious suffering.

Outside the entrance stood columns of shiny granite engraved with the faces and stories of some survivors. Stories of brutality beyond belief told a truth which any sensitive soul would want not to be so. These were testimonies of tragedy, yet in reading them I found small glimpses of hope and restored trust in humanity. Many stories spoke of barbaric acts taking place alongside the highest of human kindnesses. Despair and hope weaved through the lines of text as my watering eyes read on. My life had been so shielded from the nature and experience of mass slaughter that my mind now wrestled with wanting it not to be true.

I have no doubt the Holocaust took place. Yet at the sight of the horror that took place I can understand why some people might create a vision which reduces the real impact of the Holocaust. One man said to me that he thought the numbers of people gassed was exaggerated. As he spoke, I wondered if he was attempting to get beyond what I had felt – that of wanting it not to be true. Had the reality of what he saw moved him to construct some mitigating concept of doubt – was it really possible to kill so many people with such little gas? But to underplay any of it risks denying the truth of it all. One brutal death is one too many.

I walked slowly along the rows of granite stone, breathing in each story and studying each engraved face. Returning my gaze were seemingly familiar mothers, fathers, sisters, brothers, lovers. In a way, I saw the face of God looking back at me in the form of lives not intended to experience what they had. It surprised me how much grace and kindness seeped through each account, bearing little desire for retribution, hoping simply for an end to the possibility of this ever recurring. These personal stories brought to life people I wanted to walk and chat with, and it was as if I could hear their voices from beyond the horror they had endured.

People who were no longer one of millions but individuals with a story and a name are knowable and valuable to our own stories.

One image lodged in my mind: young Avraham Zelcer from Czechoslovakia asking a man standing next to him, "Where are the women and children?" What happened next sums up the misery. The man pointed to the chimney saying, "'They went out through there.' The only way out of Auschwitz was through the chimney: today, tomorrow, or the next day." Looking back from a place of safety and survival, Avraham wrote that it took him a year after liberation to return to his faith. *What a remarkably short time*, I thought. He lived till he was ninety-one, and had two children and twenty-one grand and great-grandchildren.

As I moved from story to story, it felt like leaving a friend. Shuffling sideways, eyes fixed forward, I read them all. Names, stories, children, and grandchildren – I wanted to honor them at least by taking the time to read what they had so graciously written. Their own words brought me into an intimacy with them and drew me into their narratives.

One name in particular, Irving Roth, stayed with me, perhaps never to leave. I lingered beyond the time it took to read, wondering if through those famous wrought iron gates I might meet Irving standing in a line.

> I was 14 years old. It was the day before Yom Kippur. I was hungry, frightened. I couldn't eat my piece of bread. I could not drink the coffee. Looking back, as a religious man, I ask myself today how did I live through this? I decided that my quarrel was not with God, but with man. It was man that created the gas chamber. Not God. In spite of all that the Nazis took from me, I made choices in the midst of this meaningless terror. I made decisions about how I would conduct myself. Faith was the only thing left. I took comfort in it.
> – Irving Roth

Irving went on to survive a death march designed to kill him. He lived till he was ninety years old. Amongst the many things he did in life, he founded a Holocaust Resource Center in New York. He also wrote a book of reflections on the Psalms.

There is little I can write here which would adequately convey the impact of standing in one of the remaining gas chambers or staring at a pile of shoes or teeth belonging to people with names and stories. None of us in our group spoke on the drive back to the hotel. Showering in cold water and dressing in fresh clothes altered nothing of the guttural cry bleeding from my heart.

I found myself in between a shattering, life-changing encounter with human misery and a lack of clarity with how to continue normal life.

We can all recognize the heavy sadness that drapes our heart when loss visits us. Our shed tears reveal what we feel – emotional emptiness. This is how I felt as though I was mourning the loss of people I had never known. What I had seen of their lives in the camps brought out a desire in me to blame someone. There are identifiable people at whose feet we can attribute responsibility, beginning likely with Hitler. But that leaves the question of how was it possible to shape the minds of millions of German people to behave so badly. Yet I sense the road of blame is a poor track down which to follow if it ends with us behaving no different to those we blame. There is a danger that we can allow the pain inflicted on us or others to govern our ongoing life. There are many stories to read of survivors who were not filled with hatred or bitterness. In one incident I read, the liberating soldiers had given some Jewish men guns to shoot their German guards with. The survivors chose not to shoot.

Who am I then to want to blame someone when I had not been the victim, merely a distant observer of history?

So I took my lead from the men and women who did survive. Overwhelmingly these people went on to put great effort into seeing that what had happened to them did not happen again. Some people were rightly found and charged and imprisoned, but in a civilized not bitter way. I'm reminded that, when Jesus said he forgave his beaters because they did not know what they were doing, he was not being naïve. They did know they were hurting him; what they did not connect with was the motivation of their actions.

I believe our spirituality can help us go beyond the immediate physical or emotional feelings the sight of injustice brings. I say this because our spirituality operates in a different way to our emotions and logic.

There are experiences in life which can touch an inner nerve from where we find ourselves with an internal scream, a wildness as it were, in our thoughts and feelings. These are raw reactions which, like the blurred scenes we see through the window of a fast-moving train, can make us unable to focus on one particular thing. Such assaults on our sensibilities can render us incapable of reasoning. We can become like an out-of-control child having a tantrum and making little sense. Before the child can be reasoned with, we might say they have to give way to the emotions which grip them. When we hear that internal scream, the rush of our emotions, we too need to find a new place of calm. Some would call it centering, others may describe "being present." Only when the rush of emotions and the acrobatics of our mind give space to the spirit within us can we make some sense of what we have encountered. This can be especially true in situations where we encounter past injustice or pain that we cannot change but need to reconcile internally.

To connect with people we have never met in the flesh yet with whom we have shared in their pain and joy, is to cross a bridge to where we feel we have truly known that person.

One friend busily talked to me about "Jack doing this" and "Jack doing that." He spoke in detail that was amazing, and for a brief moment I thought my friend Gary was talking about a friend of his and what they had gotten up to. Butting in, I said, "So who is this Jack guy and where did you two meet?" The "Jack" in question turned out to be a character named Jack Reacher, whom my friend had "met" in the pages of a fictional book. The impression of the stories of others, real or otherwise, can be so powerful!

I have another friend, a biographer, who spent many years researching and then writing the life of an historical character. During his search for information, he read diaries, visited the dead person's friends, and travelled to significant sites in the man's life. Towards the end of material gathering and on the approach to publication, the information became intimately entwined with my friend's own life and emotions. Driving along the highway one day, he burst into tears. He pulled over and sobbed a while before collecting himself. Later he would say that as he drove along it had dawned on him that he could never have a conversation with the person he had become so close to, for his subject, his friend, was dead. Having lived through the detail of his subject's life, it was as though they had shared experiences, visited places together, and developed thoughts on different subjects. On that highway that day he came to feel deep loss, a grief for a friend that in this life, in the flesh, he had never really met.

During my brief time at Auschwitz, I became connected to and moved by the lives and stories of some of the people who actually experienced the place. This filled my mind with questions, which in turn brought a powerful response.

I am not alone in this. How often do we see a news report on hunger: a bone thin face flashes before us forming a sense of human and personal connection. Immediately we might ask why or we question who is to blame as anger or sadness becomes part of this new encounter with the face and story on our screen. Right there, at the point we ask questions or start to feel something, is the beginning of a journey through which it is possible to find a moment of pause. This journey is necessary lest we become like that out-of-control child having an emotional tantrum. To make sense of the encounter which has disrupted us we need to move through and beyond the emotions to a moment of pause.

In the face of terrible things like the sight of another's pain or on hearing of an injustice it is natural to question why – to be disturbed at the level of our feeling. For some of us that disturbance is a trigger releasing anger with our God or neighbour. I believe that beyond an angry response to terrible information is something more than the Kaleidoscope of emotions rising up a storm. To pause is to move beyond our mental and emotional responses to an inner spirituality.

Accessing the spirit within is not an abandonment of pain or emotions but a point beyond where our inner reality is untouched by time and tragedy. To be angered by Auschwitz to be emotionally moved by the pain that confronts us is what makes us human. Such responses though remind us to look more closely at what we see, to listen more openly to the story before us. I believe there is a point at which we can move through and beyond to the spiritual realm where we discover the power and place of a pause.

To find a pause in the eye of a mental and emotional storm is to find where the raging wind of pain and the needle sharp rain of injustice cannot go.

There are times when the natural sensitivity of our soul brushes with the hard reality that not all people act with kindness and decency towards others.

Following my visit to Auschwitz I encountered a number of people who on the same tour of the camp came away with a different response to my own. They had seen what I had seen and read what I had read but had not sensed the moment between not knowing and knowing the detail of the horrors. For me there was a clear in-between point with a pause experience which those I talked to did not have.

I became challenged to understand why some of the people I had spoken to had seen a thousand shoes piled in a room but not equated them to five hundred knowable people. On one part of the tour through the camp are photographs of individuals who had worn those shoes. For some visitors this scene helped to move their thinking from lists and numbers to stories of individuals which in turn tapped into an emotional connection. For others the lists and numbers formed a sort of protective shield around the part of them which forges empathy. I think that the pictures of murdered Jews hung on the walls of Auschwitz are like a "soul sensitivity barometer." They move some but not all observers from knowledge about the camp to specific human connections – names and faces. Yet as one man in my home town talked of his visit to Auschwitz and the sight of the faces he said, "I pulled back before a bond was formed with another human being that I could not help."

It seems to me that in certain situations the fear of creating an emotional or mental relationship to a specific person, not just a people group, holds too much emotional risk for some. Perhaps such encounters with unthinkable terror force us to avoid thinking about the human reality. Some of us do find it less painful to look at the hard facts rather than the hurt faces.

I am not advocating for an emotional response nor rational analysis but a pathway which includes a spiritual response to. On the ride back to the hotel after my own visit to Auschwitz one young woman kept repeating, "It's so sad, it's so sad," as though her mind could not express what she felt. This reminded me of listening to a stuck record repeating the line we know whilst teasing us with the promise of a line we don't know. We know the look and feel of knowledge and we recognize the power of emotionalism, but what of the sound of spirituality in the mix as we encounter what our mind and heart cannot fully reconcile?

When I think of what it means to pause, the idea of a deeper connection with my whole being comes to mind because in pausing we are transcending the hard information, even our strong emotions, to access a more rounded reality of our wholeness.

The story in this chapter of Auschwitz tugs at the emotions, even as we are processing information. Clearly there is a connection between the mind and the emotions. Many would argue that our thoughts and feelings are one and the same thing, both functions of the brain. Yet as I have stated from the beginning, to pause is to transcend the processing of information, the seeming facts or feelings we have, to discover the spirit within us.

We all accept we are a mix of the rational and emotional approach to life. But I believe there is another part of us which completes who we are as a whole human being. We have a spirit within us which makes it possible to experience ourselves spiritually too. To know times of pause need to be part of our journey in life, a journey which involves what we think and what we feel – and our spiritual beings as well.

I have known times in my life when being confronted by injustice – the pain of a battered woman, or abused child – I simply want to cry with frustration and sadness. At times I sense that if I were to start crying, ranting or bashing things about I fear I would not find the stop button – so I hold back on the emotions!

We recognize such encounters as moments when we might change the way we see the world. A fitting phrase in *Surprised by Hope* written by Tom Wright comes to mind. "Sometimes human beings – individuals or communities – are confronted with something which they must either reject outright or which, if they accept it, will demand the remaking of their worldview."[4]

Many of our world's great movements for change began with a person becoming outraged by inequality or human suffering. First there is the lightbulb in the mind which connects the dots – we see what is actually happening. This is often followed by an emotional frustration or cry from a sense of connection with the victim or sufferer. At this moment we fear the threat of looking too closely into the eyes of Irving Roth or the faces of the abused lest that image spills over tripping untapped depths of emotion where our own pain lingers. I believe that amongst the things that can happen next is a window onto a pause. As spiritual beings we can know more than mental or emotional responses when confronted with suffering.

It is commonly known that carers can become burned out, not simply from hours worked but by the very act of caring. They enter the realm of another's suffering and begin to carry it as opposed to relieving the sufferer's pain. There is a delicate balance where we need to be close enough to the edge as it were, to see into the abyss, but not so close that we fall in.

To pause can appear at times like moving to the edge of where we would perhaps rather not be, to encounter something which is beyond our mental or emotional capacity.

Having absorbed an overstimulation of our rational processor, even becoming overwhelmed emotionally, we find ourselves knowing these two responses of our being are limited and need a break. What we don't need is more of the same, more emotion, more rationalizing. What we need is to find the off button. To pause is not to continue our thoughts or wrestle with how we feel but to move beyond to where the life of the spirit within us exists without the need of words or feelings.

Back in my hotel pacing the room, I knew I was not experiencing an emotional breakdown or losing my faith. Yet my whole being was disturbed. It occurs to me that there are transition points between the disturbance we experience and the other side of this, a little like the moment before water becomes steam or ice. We don't need a PhD in chemistry to know that there must be, however imperceptible, a moment in-between water becoming steam.

When I first visited America 20 years ago as a Brit, a good friend told me I would not find the water in the hotel hot enough to make a pot of tea; 71 Celsius is the ideal temperature. By the time I made my third visit to Chicago I gave in and left my tea bags at home and drank coffee. In a way my perfect cup of tea was just the other side of where the hotel kettle wanted to go. That is where we find an invitation to pause – not at 70 or 72 but between them. The dominance of our mind and the power of our emotions call us to rush to the other side of the journey. It is as though we can't wait for the kettle to boil but we know it must. We want the impact in our lives of spirituality now, yet any such impact only becomes evident in moments of pause, not en route.

Being confronted with the lives of people who had faced what I had not, potentially brought a new dimension to my own existence. I have come to learn that it is at times of deep connection with those who have suffered that our way forward can be influenced, often by their pain or healing, victimhood or survival. An emotional response which is normal and

45

most common, I'm told, is the work of the brain processing information, making calculations, interpreting and projecting. When we pause we are seeking a different place, stepping out of this process for a moment, not handling the pain or wrestling with the rights and wrongs but coming aside from them.

As we get to grips with what it means to have a spirit within us, a part of our being which is not subject to thoughts and emotions, we can see the profound benefit to our life of spirituality. That suffering has taken place is not removed, that our mind and heart are affected by it remains, but for a period, for a pause, we are given space – the stop button is pressed. And yes, we return perhaps to continue with the frustration and pain but our perspective has now an added dimension. I think this is what Irving Roth found when in the midst of entering and leaving the camp he said, "Faith was the only thing left. I took comfort in it." Faith is about spirituality, and spirituality is about knowing that we are more than our body and more than our thoughts.

Leaving the hotel, I walked to the Chopin Concert Hall with a flood inside of more than emotions or mental processing. A weight hung over me, a weight which was spiritual in nature. I sensed there was something beyond the capacity of my intellect or emotions. Without knowing it, we can slip away from valuing the role of the spirit within us by overreliance on the capability of our mind. We try to reconcile mentally what can only be reconciled spiritually.

Friends drawn to religious work by a desire to support the spiritual journey of others tell me that when their own spirituality becomes frayed they hit a wall. One friend told me of a time when his once-deep spirituality was pushed to one side whilst he gave spiritual guidance to others. He simply worked out of his mind and not the spirit within him. The place he had arrived at was to give out intellectual and rational counsel on spiritual issues, good in itself, but he knew his own spirituality had no depth from which to speak of spiritual matters to others.

Such thoughts crossed my mind, with this strange mix of feelings and thoughts: would I be left with a rational conclusion and spiritual emptiness? We learn on our journey that not all things are knowable nor are loose ends reconcilable. Would I lose this deep connection formed at a spiritual level with Auschwitz, a connection that I could not explain and did not create, by trying to make sense of it? Was this all an emotional overload bent on leaving me empty, drained, faithless?

The pianist that evening was Bartlomiej Kominek, a well-respected Polish musician. As he walked his fingers along the keys, the threatening force of frustration and sadness in me were parked. The music carried me far away, dancing with my soul in a way hard to describe. You will have had those moments when every now and then you sense that you have been away from the very spot you are sitting. Time has passed, but you have no idea how. It is hard to deny that such music is emotional. Looking back I can now get what the old Jewish king Saul felt when he asked David to play the harp, to soothe his troubled soul.

Sitting on the front row in that concert, a concert I didn't know would be taking place two hours before opening, I felt privileged. Not because I got the last ticket or that the organizer put me at the front. Privileged because in this space my soul found a pausing place. Here I parked the grappling questions of injustice and sadness, frustration and cruelty. This pause allowed me to mourn for the people I had not known in this life but encountered at the deeper level of my own humanity.

Each keystroke of the pianist lifted and massaged my mourning heart. Halfway through the hour-long recital, I quietly wept for Irving – for his parents and siblings leaving Auschwitz through the chimney. I wept for the families of the German guards years later having to reconcile what uncle Heinrich or granddad Franz had done to the Jews in those camps. Etty

Hillesum, known for her spiritual diaries, wrote not long before her death in Auschwitz, "I shall have to pray for this German soldier. Out of all those uniforms one has been given a face now. There will be other faces, too, in which we shall be able to read something we understand: that German soldiers suffer as well. There are no frontiers between suffering people, and we must pray for them all."[5] Benjamin Watson the American football player writes in his book *Under Our Skin* of an occasion when he filled out a form which asked for his race. He checked the box "other." He writes, "Not because I'm not proud of my skin color, my ancestry, or my heritage, because I am. I checked 'other' because I know that the real humanity, the soul and spirit under our skin, is what makes us who we are." In the space to identify what we mean by "other"[6] Benjamin wrote – HUMAN.

I believe that the more we become acquainted with and engaged around the spirit within us the less we are taken up with what divides us. Clearly it was that they were and are in touch with the spirit that is within which enabled Etty Hillesum and enables Benjamin Watson to see beyond the mortal framework we present to one another and into the spirit that is within every one.

As Bartlomiej paused on the last depression of the keys, letting the notes stroke the air, I felt a flood of thanksgiving wash through me. Whilst everyone waited for a long moment before standing to applaud, the voice of Irving Roth came flooding into my soul. "Faith was the only thing left. I took comfort in it."

There are times and situations which we can neither change nor turn off but from which we need to emerge with relief. To not find a moment of pause can leave us feeling trapped behind a door with no obvious handle while at the center of a storm. You and I are changed less by what information we gather, perhaps even less by emotional disruption, yet at the center of the gathering we can discover a transforming pause. I wonder if through encounters at the deeper level of humanity we form connections with the world beyond our sight. Did I really meet Irving Roth that day? Can it be possible that our spirituality has such potential depth that physical presence is less important than soulful connection?

In life, we encounter situations where we journey to the edge of many things, perhaps even an abyss of tears. Could it be that in our sensitive seeking of a spirituality we encounter something beyond the numbers and dimensions of what we see? Over the years I have discovered that a pause by nature not intention or design will often result in a gain of perspective. I wonder if the pauses that have the greatest impact on our journey take place at the deepest encounters and the richest connections.

Maybe when you next think you can't switch off or possibly carry any more new information, when the emotions are running on overdrive, try *not* looking for the exit. Imagine if we chose not to push away an encounter or rush on to the next, but to stop at the in-between place. Imagine if we were to pause at the transition from one to the next!

In that I believe we will put breath into the sentences of our own story. We won't change the world, but by finding a place of pause we may be changed ourselves.

Pause

Chapter 4

Making room for the three elements of our being

The train from Quetta to Lahore took more than twenty-four hours in blistering heat with nothing wet or cool to dampen the skin for comfort. The water tank above the carriage was boiling, too hot to drink, probably unwise to try even if cold. A fuller train I could not imagine. Filling the space around me were boxes, hessian sacks, a goat, and two chickens.

Approaching the outskirts of Sukkur where we would cross the Indus River, a palpable buzz filled the air as people shuffled bags in preparation for the station. To the average Westerner, it was utter chaos as people moved in every direction. Yet to the locals it seemed perfectly natural behavior. I sat thinking it would all settle. It didn't. Braving the door and swimming through the sea of bodies, I reached the platform in search of a cold drink. Sweat leaked from every pore, leaving me dehydrated and holding a thirst that felt unquenchable. From a platform seller I bought half a watermelon which melted onto my tongue and oiled my throat – relief. It hit the spot like a warm bath on a cold day, altering my body temperature to comfortable.

Wanderlust and youth had drawn me into the heart of Pakistan en route to India from the UK. The year was 1984, and I was braving the challenge to cross continents low-budget style. Multilinguists are hard to find in remote places, so you remain separated from the culture. It's here where you are the foreigner, the outsider, appearing to others as somewhat exotic, even viewed as questionable. I used my hands to communicate.

As I reboarded the train, I felt fatigued, and I could tell sickness was in my body. Yet I was determined: I would press on. I could put off my need for rest and restoration until an undetermined tomorrow in the future. Anyone that has ever battled with an extra few pounds around the waist will know that tomorrow never comes – as Elvis Presley sang to his adoring fans, "It's now or never... tomorrow will be too late."

On my journey, I found that, at the same time as my sickness took me captive, my spiritual wellness nosedived into a weariness of its own. The basis of this book requires us to accept that we are more than our body and more than our thought, that our wholeness includes the active presence of the spirit within us. During my travels, I began to consider my exploration into the relationship between the three elements of our being. Nearing the Indian border, as you will read, my spiritual and physical needs were both met in the same space and time but only after I had overcome my mental resistance to the idea of stopping. I needed to end the pushing of my need towards an imaginary tomorrow.

The sun lowered towards the horizon as I sat in the open doorway of the train, feet dangling and my body cooling with the breeze. Jalal, a young man my age, joined me with the intention of practicing his English. He began probing with questions which brought out our shared interest in faith. As a Christian, he was an anomaly within his own country and was under constant threat of being singled out for ill treatment. We struck a note of shared spiritual hope and talked animatedly, a simple joy along the journey, yet a challenge to my growing sense of overall malaise.

Jalal picked up that I was not entirely well or able to get comfortable. Most of our fellow travellers were used to being in very close seating, packed in like sardines in a tin can. This wasn't working for me, and so my new friend encouraged those around me to move, and they did. For the first time in my 5,500-mile overland journey, while I still felt ill, at least now I was more comfortable. In truth I had not slept properly for some ten days, being constantly on the move as I crossed Turkey, Iran, and now Pakistan. Attempts to exercise my spirituality, to meditate and pray, had proved tough, and my sickness, I sensed, was more than just physical.

Nothing I ate or drank remained inside my body. Life slowly drained from me with each visit to the bathroom where that boiling tap water and pungent smell rising from the toilet bowl added to my malaise. At that moment, in that carriage of a hot train, I just wanted to be somewhere else.

It is clear to me now that despite how awful physically, mentally, and spiritually I felt, the drive to get to New Delhi, the next contact point on my journey, was immovable. This need to get to my next port of call overrode any present reality I was experiencing.

Sometimes we have within us such a deep sense of destiny that we can see only the goal. We form a crystal-clear image in our thinking of what is upfront, ahead, over the next hill, an image all-consuming. Engaging with others or contemplating breaking off from the trajectory we are following can at times come into conflict with this sense of destiny and inner urge to achieve or reach our reckless pursuit.

The hardest taskmaster can be self. At times we lack compassion for our own well-being. This can come out in underestimating our actual circumstance.

I read once of a man who ran full pelt for several minutes across a battlefield towards a safe line of trees. During those minutes he was unaware that a large part of his thigh had been blown out. He stopped only because he heard a squelching noise and looked down to see his boot full of blood. There are situations when what is imagined to be up ahead overrides what is true in the present, which in the instance of this man possibly saved his life.

What keeps us going is that we are not in the present but living beyond the moment as it were focused on a future event or place. This ability to keep moving forward does have limits. That soldier would have bled to death eventually, a depression can become a breakdown, and our spirituality can run aground for lack of investment.

Picture one of those moments when we are away from home and our health dips below par – it is a horrible and even frightening feeling. My wife once took ill in Kenya. We hesitated to call the doctor, thinking in a week we could see our own doctor back at home. Thankfully, we didn't put it off, and she received amazing care from a local doctor right then and there – in the present, not some dreamt-up future convenient moment. We can find ourselves conflicted – the body wants to stop and close the eyes, but the mind is pushing on.

The truth is we often plan to deal with present needs in a future place or time. It is as though we long to be anywhere but where we are, putting present needs on hold whilst battling with conscious awareness of those needs. In my case, I needed to experience stillness, to pause, to rest and to receive.

One place we can experience a sense of stillness, an inner peace where we step away from conscious concern for ourselves, is when we are in deep sleep, dead to the world, as my mother would say. There is, however, an internal conflict in which stopping to rest butts up against wanting to choose the terms of that rest. I'm reminded of childhood car journeys with my dad. We would ask, "When can we stop?" Looking over his shoulder he would say, "When we get there." I'm sure he too had a need for a rest, but he had decided ahead at which junction he'd stop, not when and where his kids needed a toilet.

I believe that the physical, spiritual, and mental elements of our lives are at times unhelpfully viewed as independent of each other. I remember one day a friend asked me if the tiredness I told him I felt was a warning sign of declining mental health. He'd asked me how I felt not what I had been up to – which was a ninety mile cycle ride the day before. I was physically tired.

Like so many of us my friend wanted to isolate a part of my being so a fix could be brought in. This can be helpful but leads to compartmentalizing.

I have said in this book that we are more than our thoughts and more than our bodies, that we are spirit too. In this chapter I am expressing that those three elements have a depth of interaction which sometimes defies our understanding.

My Buddhist friends might argue that these three are faces of one entity, and that none is the vessel or captain of the other. For me, that's quite a helpful image and encourages the idea that these three aspects of who I am are entwined, related, even on occasion in concert.

Many of us can find our mind resisting recognition that we are physically unwell when in fact we are. A close friend suffers from depression but I notice that her friends see it coming on long before she does. It is as though we have an inability to accept our fallibility in these areas.

I believe it is equally true of our spirituality. We can sense or know that our spirituality is under par yet there is a lag in responding. Dullness to the spirit within us can creep in to even the most spirituality-minded person.

I have heard a number of praying people say when they sense a real connection with their God, their prayers reach far into the universe; but other times, it is as though their prayers are only hitting the ceiling. I learned in Pakistan that there are occasions when there comes a moment when we are physically unhealthy, spiritually opaque, and mentally finding no traction. It is as though life as we know it in the physical, mental, or spiritual sense is not regenerating us. This is when our greatest need is for our whole being to be in concert, not the mind overriding the body or the body overruling the spirit within us.

Is it possible that this resistance to life in the present is born of our desire to be in the future, on the move, looking into tomorrow from today?

My experience in Pakistan was just what I described, a convergence of pressure on the whole of my being. I had a clear physical need for my body to rest and an unrealistic, irrational mental desire to press on despite an undernourished, neglected spirituality. We can find ourselves pushing on and hoping to get through to some imaginary right moment – but we need an intervention or we will crash.

Let's suggest this is another one of those invitations to pause, to release the dominant grip of the mind and body, to give room for the spirit within us.

Arriving at Lahore train station, Jalal, my newfound friend, invited me back to his home. He gestured a head-on-a-pillow sign. He was telling me to rest. I resisted the suggestion, thinking I should press on to the India border. I had a contact in New Delhi where I might find a place to rest up, if I could just make it there. Standing, convincing myself not to stop, I had no idea that in two days' time I would need all the strength and wit I could muster.

Unbeknown to me the Indian army were amassing troops around Amritsar ready to attack the holiest shrine of Sikhism, the Golden Temple. They did so on the very day that I crossed the border and entered the area in conflict. I found myself at the heart of the chaos and fighting, and needing to be alert and able to run quickly. Neither of which I could do had I pressed on that day.

Thankfully the fight left me. Forty minutes later, we stepped off the bus we had caught from outside the train station and walked to his home. Along his street were open sewers, dust, and noise, which did nothing to lift my weakened body.

Floods of children came up to us wanting to engage and touch me, talk to me and tease me, and I just wanted the world to stop. The area we were in, Youhanabad, is a predominantly Christian population. Over the years, attacks and killings had plagued the neighborhood.

Jalal's family were poor, poorer than anyone I had ever met before. Their home was a rectangular, single-story, sandy-colored building typical of that part of the world. Its tin roof covered a third of the property, leaving a yard for cooking and for living during the day.

This little humble family welcomed me as a son and busily shared all they had. The inside of the house, underneath the tin roof, was stiflingly hot. As night fell, Jalal brought his father's bed out to the yard. Try as I might to explain I could not take the aged man's bed, he insisted. I couldn't insult their kindness, so I accepted. (We are so often blown away by the immense generosity of the poorest people. It seems to me their kindness is drawn from a well of grace, of honest empathy.)

I wonder if our resistance to letting go of that perfect future moment in our sights is because deep down we sense our current need to be beyond a short-term fix. I'm sure I had in mind that in New Delhi I would rest and refresh for weeks not hours. That day I learned to accept what was offered me without comparing it to what I imagined I might have in the future.

A prophet of old, Elisha, encouraged a widow in debt and told her to take what little oil she had and start pouring into empty jars. The story is that more jars were filled than her imagination could conceive would be. I feared that a physical, even emotional, rest would not suffice, so I held back from even being willing to lay on an offered bed. Shakespeare wrote, "Weary with toil, I haste me to my bed, The dear repose for limbs with travel tired; But then begins a journey in my head." He speaks of the fitful night and broken sleep, for while the body lays down the mind fights on. It's much the same in meditation. We position ourselves for a period of calm, almost thoughtlessness, and then the mind fills with worry and wondering. Our job, family, life mission all take a higher place vying for attention insistent that switching off, pausing, will rob us of life.

The complete opposite is true.

I read an article titled "The Power of Restorative Sleep" which suggested our well-being, even some minor ailments, can be dealt with through a form of deep sleep. The idea here is akin to a complete shutdown of our mental processes, coma-like. This is not to say that prayers and pills don't work, but that there is the possibility that a halting from cognitive and physical activity may help. The question then arises what is left if the mind and body are on a break? I believe in such a situation the spirit within us has greater room to move, to breathe and exercise spiritual life.

Do you ever marvel that a surgical team can take a failing heart out of a person and replace it with a donor's healthy heart? You lie on the table induced into a deep sleep and eight hours later your chest is being stapled shut, and it is as though you were not present. With some head injuries, doctors place a patient into a medically-induced coma. They do this to allow the body to rest and recuperate, and for the brain to enter a temporary state of hibernation. People who suffer from anxiety, which affects breathing, digestion, and even decision making, find that an unbroken fit-less sleep has the power to reset a particular bout of attacks.

In Youhanabad, Lahore, I looked set for the worst night's sleep ever. The bed was a charpai, wooden framed with rope-like woven material which formed the bit you lie on. It looked very uncomfortable. This one was old and had a fair sag in the middle which my weight put more pressure on than the old man's. Jalal's father had given up one of the few possessions he owned to help put a break in my relentless pressing ahead. As I lowered myself onto the bed in the cool of the night I saw more stars than I had ever noticed before. Then as if a light switch were turned off, I entered an inexplicable unconsciousness.

Looking back to that night, I realize I had arrived at a moment in my life when I was physically drained and spiritually in a wilderness. My mind, as is often the case, took control and created a narrative which placed an immense pressure on me to reach New Delhi before considering creating any space for rest or regeneration. This driven sense of destiny seemed to override the cries of protest to stop, rest, and restore that my body and my spirit were making.

When eventually I *did* stop, I went beyond sleep into what I can only describe as a form of hibernation, a shutting down of the body and mind.

It has been my fortune in life to have never needed to be put in an induced coma but this experience had all the hallmarks of one. What did not stop or shut down was the activity of the spirit within me. As I have said elsewhere, our spirituality is not governed or controlled by our emotions, our mind or a body. Our spirituality exists without need of food or a good book to stimulate the spirit within us.

That night without the aid or comfort of drips or drugs, duvets or air conditioning, my entire being – body, mind and spirit – paused. It was as though a reset button had been hit. Although I was consciously unaware, a balance was being restored to the members of my being.

It would be a gross understatement to simply say I had a good night's sleep. I awoke physically well – healed, mentally positive, without anxiety, full of optimism and spiritually alive, things that many of my good night's sleeps since have never brought in the morning.

The sounds of the city waking up and the smell of smoke gently brought me round with ten hours having passed. This great pause had restored me. In letting go of the urge to leave off addressing my present needs to the future, in New Delhi, I had listened to my whole being cry, "Stop!" My physical, spiritual, and mental life encountered a level of restoration only possible when all three accepted and entered a moment of pause in concert with one another. Hot tea, warm chapati and a mint dip reawakened me in a way I could not describe, filling my now hungry stomach.

I was invited to attend morning prayers, which led to my speaking at a gathering of local Christians later that evening. I realized that without the time of pause the night before, I would not have physically, spiritually, or mentally been able to address these wonderful people. It was the first time I had been asked to speak in a public meeting about faith and spirituality. I was a novice, a newcomer and yet I found a niche in which to fit. Thirty-seven years on and I still look back at that moment when the energized and enthusiastic young me shared thoughts of the spiritual life with a group of Pakistani Christians. It was in some ways a catalyst or launch for my life of spiritual encounter in a public way with others.

My night in Lahore was a time of disengaging with the world around me, not just a sleep but more a separation from all that influenced me. Yes, it was a dreamless and inexplicable coma-like night, yet one that left me with the sense I had had communion with the creator and the creation. My mind and body may have appeared sleeping, but the spirit within me was alive, awake and active.

The morning after the night of pause I woke spiritually, mentally, and physically alive in a way I could not nor needed to explain. In the part of the world I was in spiritual teachers use the phrase "getting beyond our rational consciousness to experience the divine mystery." Is this longhand for "pause" I wonder?

Consider what a difference it might make if you respond not by shrugging off the cry to rest but accepting that call for pause.

In pause, you lay down your concern for tomorrow and allow your body, mind, and the spirit within to rest and restore together.

Pause

Part Two

Having located the doorway, you now need to step into the sanctuary.[7]

Making Room for It, Creating It, Listening for It

Chapter 5

Looking for Pause in All the Right Places

Our youngest daughter was still ten years away from saying quiet countryside time with us was no longer the cool thing to do. In those days we knew the uncertainty of our finances would make having regular relaxed time away from our busy work difficult if at all possible. Mark, a close family relative, agreed to join with us in pooling resources so to afford us all a getaway home. With our combined but modest budget we were able to buy a used mobile home on a remote and small park in Wales.

The owner of Penddol Park was gracious at the sight of our limited funds, and he sold us a mobile home that was earmarked for the breakers yard (scrap heap) at the end of that season. Generous, but not soft in business, Graham made it clear we could use the mobile home for two years and then we had to upgrade for a newer, tidier-looking model. Our first job was to have a sign made, which we hung over the door, and from that moment forward it was no longer a mobile home but "Willows Rest."

It was surprising to us how soon we felt at home there, relaxed, even familiar with its sounds and smells. Have you ever noticed the marked difference in how quickly we can chill out in places familiar to us? Wherever I have been on my travels, a long drive or flight, holiday or business, nothing seems as physically and emotionally comforting as our family home.

I have noticed this on a spiritual level too. I have visited some awe-inspiring structures, including the Taj Mahal, the Grand Mosque, and many Cathedrals, yet as well designed and seemingly spiritual as they were, I found a deeper, easier spiritual access at Willows Rest. Over time, as you will read, this small mobile home became an in-between place, a sort of break in the events of our lives. I would go on to describe Willows Rest not as a home from home but as a home for my soul. Strange I know, but it is possible to identify a place where our inner being finds less resistance in the journey towards moments of pause.

To mitigate the peril of Graham's sword of Damocles hanging over poor Willows Rest, we planted colorful border flowers and used foliage to disguise its aged look. It was a mini makeover. Most folk at Penddol were in a similar position, working in jobs that paid okay but not enough for a villa in Spain. The two years came and went with no comment from our friendly landlord – he must have put the sword down! After four years we painted Willows Rest a newer-looking green, and I built a better-looking wooden set of steps. We improved the front of our plot. Graham never mentioned his original instruction for us to buy something newer within two years. After six years of our being there, he sold Penddol Park and left.

The new owner, Llynne, was a lovely man with a kind heart. It was his first Holiday Park and we suspected that he had intended it to be a retirement project. The work of managing and site maintenance and the growing legal changes to swimming pools and recreation areas proved more work than he first anticipated. But he smiled through it all. He was one of those people who liked his toys, so he bought a big digger and a sit-on lawnmower. It was fun getting to know him.

Over the years I have read with envy about those people fortunate enough to have funds to buy a farm or mountain and create an idyllic retreat. Although what we had created was tenuous, on the edge of our budget, just a shared doorway to some countryside, it was ours. It was not a remote hidden retreat where supplies are flown in and the mountain water is clear and fresh. Our near neighbors were twenty meters not twenty kilometers away. Yet it was away from our norm, and that was the key. We discovered that it is possible to find or create a space, an ordinary space filled with ordinary people, which became a place of spiritual encounter.

In his second year as site owner, and our eighth as tenants, Llynne mentioned that Willows Rest needed changing. We told him we couldn't afford a replacement. A little sadness rested over us as we began to think about leaving.

A day after our conversation he said to us that we would be surprised at what we could afford. We were bowled over by his response. How could he know what we had or didn't have in the bank!

Soon after that conversation one late sunny September day, as we returned from a long walk with our dog, Llynne asked us to look at a thirty-two foot mobile home he had sitting in the main parking area. Walking past it earlier that day, we had assumed it had been bought and was waiting to be sited. We had looked at it with envy.

Encouraged by Llynne to take the key and look around the mobile home, we did and fell in love with it. It was that kind of feeling you get when you trade up your car and find heated seats and a screen demister that actually works! We explained we simply didn't have the funds. He offered to take Willows Rest on her final journey to the breakers yard free of charge and put the replacement in the space; the only outlay to us would be the installation cost and the year's ground rent, which we would normally pay anyway. Such generosity.

Over the years we found ourselves having some wonderful breaks at Willows Rest. On many occasions during these times of rest we discovered it to be a place of pause too. I recall a number of Friday afternoons when we drove away from our place of work with a head full of pain, fear, frustration – only to find it all fading as we arrived at Penddol Park. We would frequently enjoy a few days simply sitting outside, watching the birds nest or the young lambs frolicking.

One such afternoon as I observed the bark on a tree the most amazing thing happened.

Perfectly blended in with the browns and greens of the bark and moss, moving upward was a small Treecreeper. A slender little bird, brown speckled on its back and white on the front. Its curved long bill pointing down was tugging away at something which eventually became the bird's dinner. What struck me most was that it moved up the tree just a few inches then stopped. It would poke around and after a while move on. This went on inch by inch to the top of the trunk, a slight movement and stop, slight movement and stop. At each stop another insect or spider was drawn from a crevice to become sustenance. This little Treecreeper was completely alone, away from its nest.

I thought about how important it is, to come away from home and feed on what can't be found in our normal setting. The Treecreeper would leave behind an empty foodless crevice in the bark, albeit a few inches away, to arrive at another feeding place. I knew then the importance of being somewhere that felt like a spiritual feeding station.

That was the day I realized that Willows Rest provided for us a place for pause.

Here we could pause in the midst of a busy life and sometimes, spiritually speaking, move from an empty feeding station to a full one. Here, we found a space to stop for a while and move on. Unknowingly and unintentionally we had created somewhere to go and experience a measure of sanctuary and solitude. Under two hours' drive from our home we had a haven, a harbor into which we could weigh anchor when needed. It was a privilege.

In some ways Willows Rest might have been described as an entry point or place of threshold, as some would describe, to the spiritual realm. This term "threshold" is used to speak of a point where two worlds meet, or where the point of crossing takes place. More often than not this is the image used of the space in between heaven and earth, the life beyond our sight.

William Blake is often attributed with the line, "In the universe, there are things that are known, and things that are unknown, and in between them, there are doors." I suspect that over the centuries we humans have romanticized or fantasized about this point of crossover, the threshold of the door. In his book *Constantine's Sword*, James Carroll recounts a pivotal moment for him on a visit to Israel. At the age of thirty he came across the threshold stone which lay at one of the gates into the city of Jerusalem in the time of Jesus. He was immediately struck by the knowledge that Jesus, when standing on that step, was not in the city of his death nor out of it, he was in-between.

I wonder if he paused!

Many popular films have storylines which hang on the idea of a threshold, an in-between place, a portal if you will. Film portals can be amazingly elaborate at times. A hero or villain passes through this mysterious opening to do good or ill. The 1994 science fiction movie *Stargate* had a huge metal ring which connected to a similar one in another part of the universe, not unlike H.G. Wells' *Time Machine*, which transported the main character back or forward in time. How often have we pondered the idea that whilst we are here in the present reality, we could be in another place or at least look through the door to it? If not you, then a child you know will have moved aside the coats hanging in a wardrobe to test the back, hoping for a door into Narnia.

Willows Rest was not as elaborate as the Time Machine or the Stargate and no lamppost or talking fawn could be found in the wardrobe, but it was a place which increased our capacity or openness to the realm of the spiritual. In some way it was where we poked through to moments of pause. It became a place of threshold where we seemed to move more easily beyond the constraints of our ordinary material and mental concerns. As I said earlier, it was more than simply a home-from-home, for it held an added sense of spiritual openness. It was a place where my spirit could stand on a threshold or enter a door which revealed spiritual refreshment in a way I was not finding at home.

In his book *The Way of the Heart*, Henri Nouwen makes the statement that, "We have to fashion our own desert place..."[8] He goes on to describe this desert place as one to which we withdraw into the presence of God. Although his imagery is a desert, his point is a matter of spirituality. What an intriguing idea it is to recognize that we can create or identify a space where the possibility of a richer spiritual encounter is heightened.

I think of the line, "Draw near to God and God will draw near to you." It is a bit like wanting to see the stars while remaining inside the house – we might not leave the house but will need to have a seat nearer the window so as to look out and up. It is a move away from the distractions at the center of the room – TV, books, pictures on the wall. You aren't guaranteed to see the stars from the window – it might be cloudy – but you definitely won't see them away from the window. You move to increase the possibility. It's part of what Nouwen is saying in the words, "We have to withdraw..."

There are times and circumstances in life when the events and pressures of life so assault us that we would welcome the seclusion a desert might offer. The idea of living in a desert may sound extreme, but no doubt there are times when a desert-like place can be appealing. We humans have hidden in deserts for centuries because generally no one else wants to be there, which makes it a place that can feel safe.

As a young boy I was once being chased by some older lads and I ran into the middle of a shallow but muddy river. I knew they had nice clothes on and I guessed right they would not follow me in, which created a space and some time for me to calm down a little.

Henri Nouwen was reflecting on the Desert Mothers and Fathers, early Christians whose extreme search for seclusion and a measure of safety was to purposely find a distant and therefore difficult-to-reach place. Their quest was for separation from a world of temptation, indifference, and distraction. In a way their desert represented the muddy river for me, a place where those who might harm or interrupt their journey were reluctant to go. (Of course they were on a lifelong spiritual journey whereas I was simply trying to get home from school safely!)

It is interesting that a desert place can be seen as sanctuary to hide in or seclusion to spiritually thrive in. The thread of Nouwen's suggestion is not essentially about running from trouble but fashioning a space (desert) where we, "… dwell in the gentle healing presence of *God*."[9] Those early Christians who chose to make their home in the desert and to build communities of prayer and silence were not running *from* something as much as they were running *to* something. They were seeking a richer encounter with the spirit within them and on to their God. I believe they were creating a place in which to stimulate access to moments of pause, to enter the interior life within and to touch if not enter the threshold of what they would describe as the presence of God.

I accept that the desert remains a place of limited comforts regardless of whether sought for refuge or privacy. Forced by circumstance or sought by personal need, finding or creating a desert place in our lives is more like weighing an anchor in calm waters than tying off on a busy dockside. We are not looking for the supplies store and the amenities of a seaside town, rather we are looking for basic shelter and seclusion. I wonder if the comfort of our lives, the ease of access to abundant resources, the distractions of entertainment, might be a limiting factor in our desire for the kind of ascetic seclusion the desert seemed to offer those early spiritual seekers. In the way that Henri Nouwen's thoughts are about withdrawing to a less distracting and more simplistic place I can see how Willows Rest became this for us.

James Martin, a Jesuit, makes the point that we are today by and large in cultures where simplicity and voluntary poverty are almost opposed by the predominance of materialism. He reflects on a spiritual life which centers on poverty, chastity, and obedience. "In a culture that celebrates money, sex, and freedom a life which is seeking spirituality through simplicity is not only irrelevant but a threat."[10] I have friends who would choose not to book a perfectly good holiday cottage simply because it has poor Wi-Fi. We cannot deny that the lack of comfort we find when away from our familiar family homes may make the opportunity for a getaway, the opportunity for pause, less attractive.

Many of us have surrounded ourselves with *stuff* that serves our material wants and needs, making it uncomfortable to even imagine being in a place where we have chosen to give up some of those comforts. Presently we turn on a tap and let it run cold before putting the glass under for a drink. Our refrigerator is full and the supermarket is in sight. Not so in the desert where the limited water supply takes on a new value. We are told that the body can survive without food for up to sixty days, yet remove water and our days are reduced to a handful.

The Desert Mothers and Fathers saw no value in dying of dehydration or starvation. Instead, they discovered that in the limited availability of supplies and in the separation from what may previously have been thought of as essential, they found a route to a more spiritually focused life. They recognized we have an over-occupation with the material aspect of living. Once again, I remind myself, we are more than our body and more than our thoughts.

I see in the Desert Mothers and Fathers people seeking almost complete abandonment of wider society. It didn't work because they were followed and communities grew around them. Over time these communities moved back toward cities and towns, and we see the rise of Monasteries. These were an attempt to have the simplified secluded life that the Mothers and Fathers had had but without the desert.

Whether in the desert caves or town monastery they were seeking to create a place of threshold for spirituality, or a gateway to, as some refer to it, the "interior life." They – in fact you and I – have remained engaged with the wider world whilst looking for a way to nurture or give room for the spirit within us to breathe. In a way I can see how our Willows Rest was in this line of desert places and monasteries. It is not *where* but *what* takes place which determines what Nouwen called, "A desert place."

There comes a point in our journey towards a richer spirituality when we have established our cave in the desert, our Willows Rest in the countryside, or even a chair by the window. We become less distracted by our material, even emotional, needs.

When we identify our desert place, we enter another challenge. So much of who we perceive ourselves to be loses relevance in a desert place because our normal frames of reference are removed. There is no requirement on us to do anything other than to simply be. At first we might arrive at our desert place and settle into quietness or reflection. It is a space like any other, yet it is where we hope to spend time in spiritual pursuit. As we take tentative steps forward in this journey we discover spirituality is not reached when we sit in our cave or special chair but when we step over the fence of our preoccupied thoughts. We have to learn to be satisfied with nothing more than the moment and place we are in.

Much of what I have expressed here has been focused on the setting of the desert, monastery, and mobile home which is important but they are not the actual spiritual encounter. Once we find ourselves alone in our "desert place" we might rightly sense a desire for spirituality. Yet here, our experience can become one of frustration – something should happen and that something is not happening. External distractions held at bay leave us with the internal distraction of the mind. In the teachings of the Desert Mothers and Fathers is recognition that one of the greatest distractions is not always what we withdraw from or arrive at on a physical level but what we bring with us – our internal dialogue.

My wife and I foster dogs on their way from an unpleasant environment to a good home. Some of these dogs spend hours in the doorway between the room with their bed and food and our family room. They can't settle in either so they are in both, sometimes prowling back and forth coming and going in and out. That is how our mind can work seeking permission to rest but not knowing where or how.

I have learnt that a desert place is where there is no need for a decision or direction of thought. There is a strange vulnerability about this; it is as though there is a need to let go of something. Often in these situations I think I should be doing something, making something happen; you may recognize this. So familiar are we with the stimulation of food for our bodies and information for our minds that when the opportunity comes to release the tightness of our grip on these things, we panic as though not trusting that there is anything more to us than body and mind.

Imagine seeing a young swimmer taking her first high dive in a pool. She looks apprehensive, and you can almost hear her calculating the distance to the water, the speed at which she will fly, and the impact. Her face is serious, a reflection of her racing thoughts. Standing on the edge, her hesitancy of mind translates to her curling toes as she grips the dive platform. Moments later, grinning ear to ear, she reappears from beneath the water, eager to climb the ladder and go again. For her the thrill of the dive occurs between her thoughts while standing on the board and her physical experience of entering the water. A moment of pause, an encounter with the spirit within us, is not a physical body experience and it is not a set of intellectual thoughts. It is that moment in-between when the spirit within us has room to soar.

Arriving at a desert place we can easily enter an internal dialogue: "What should I be doing, what should I be thinking?" We can move back and forth, weighing up when and how to enter the spiritual realm, standing as if on the edge of a diving board. The image of a desert is simply a place which becomes the ground from which we enter a moment of pause. It is here that the existence of a deeper, some may say divine connection, becomes a matter of finally letting go, including of our racing thoughts. When we are sitting in our cave, it becomes our desert place when we unfurl our curled-up toes and stop mentally working out every detail of life's journey. It is then we enter pause.

One of the most well-known of the Desert Fathers is Anthony the Great who lived in the second century. John Wortley writes of how Anthony sought solitude in three different places before settling. It seems one of his great challenges was to find a place he could exercise his desire for time alone whilst remaining part of the wider religious community. This became evident when after thirteen years of remote living an illness forced him to accept the help he needed from others. Once well again Anthony retreated back to the desert alone for a short while before, "A community developed in association with Anthony's retreat."[11] The life and experience of Anthony is a reminder that our desert place is not a deserted place but a place we encounter points of spiritual access.

The Desert Mothers and Fathers are unfortunately named so because of where they practiced their spirituality. The actual desert part is much less important than the spirituality they discovered in themselves whilst in the desert. The suggestion of Henri Nouwen is that the desert or the physical environment we use is a facilitation for bringing us closer to a deeper spiritual encounter.

The Desert Fathers' and Mothers' caves were not temporary living spaces like my mobile home or a friend's spare room. Clearly we don't all have to live in an actual desert to find a place from where we experience less resistance to spiritual encounter and moments of pause.

I often think about that little Treecreeper away from the nest, taking regular stops on its way up the trunk feeding little but often with many short, high-impact breaks. I think of how we find it really helpful in our walk of spirituality to have a desert place which might be our version of stops along the tree. Many of us work solidly for long periods, broken only with short breaks. As welcome as these breaks are, I suspect that the spirit within us, as the Desert Mothers and Fathers discovered, is better served when we dwell in a space for some time, where we can find the realm of our spirituality closer to the surface.

Making time to be away from your day-to-day world, your norm, into a place you have chosen, a place where you can move more easily beyond the constraints of your ordinary concerns, is a way of inviting pause. This will become your desert place. You can find the possibility of a richer spiritual encounter greatly heightened by purposely seeking out seclusion and solitude.

So might I ask you, "Where's your desert place?"

Pause

Chapter 6

Creating Pause in a Busy Life

There was a time when watching TV required preparation. I remember those days disconnecting the phone, lining up the kettle and cups, ready for the interval. You might have to wait twenty or more minutes before a loo break or risk missing the punch line or murder clue! These were days, and not so long ago, when we didn't have control over the start time, break time, or end time of entertainment. To not be on the couch at 7:30pm guaranteed you missed the start. There were annoying interruptions. The sound of the toilet flushing immediately followed by a panicky, "What happened, what happened?" by the sibling who just couldn't have waited another ten minutes!

Many years later my nine-year-old grandson paused our watching of *Home Alone* to have a brief conversation with his mum on the phone. This was followed by his nipping to the toilet before returning to the couch. Using that now so familiar button, with two lines on, he managed not to miss a single frame of the film. On occasions he stops a film partway through and returns to it on his next visit maybe a week later. Fortunately, like many young folk, our grandson can remember the storyline for weeks and has no need of the rewind button.

Separated by five decades, these two film-watching experiences prompted me to question whether the pause button makes me lazier and less disciplined about my time. Of course it has its upside too. I can now choose to spend my ten or so waking hours doing the things I want in the order I choose without slotting into a broadcaster's time frame.

That said, because so much of life can now be done when we choose, there is a sense that our choices are now more important. In some way, of the things we have less control over we have to be more intentional about them. Hence you need to be sitting in front of the TV at a specific time or you will miss the show! Nowadays with our on-demand, "when-do-you-want-it-to-happen-sir," world we can take it or leave it, do half now, half later. I recognize there are some major advantages to this kind of control over the things we do. Yet I can't help thinking this can lead to us being less focused, less available to the experience of life.

A stop-start experience of anything will change the nature of how we engage with whatever the thing is.

Looking back on those film-watching experiences of me and my father, and my grandson and me, is an image many of us are familiar with. In the 1970s our family would gather together in one room to watch a film. Today we can all stream the same film at the same time and be in different rooms or houses, even continents. As a child the only thing I streamed was a cold, and watching a film with my dad involved lots of being abruptly told to not talk, "Be quiet and tell me that later." Later of course never came.

The advantage of the pause button has been to create space to talk or put our attention somewhere else.

Along with all illustrations the TV pause button has limits yet it serves as a reminder that there are moments when we know that what we are doing at a specific instance is less important than an emerging desire. The pause button reminds us that there are things we can put on hold whilst we make ourselves available for something else. The pause button reminds us that things will still be there when we return to play. Imagine we go to bed at night and draw the curtains closed. On awakening in the morning we draw back the curtains and unsurprisingly the world has seldom changed. Even an overnight snow covering doesn't change the layout of our garden; the pile of old bricks we planned to move still awaits our attention. So it is when we have identified an invitation to still the background noise and soften the external demands in life in order to move nearer to the realm of the spirit within us.

We might ask then, what does a pause mean for us in our daily lives? How long will we give to the breaks in the other things of life which occupy us? To think with the constraints of time in mind is to miss the point. When John Newton wrote the song *Amazing Grace* he put a flaw in one of the lines, "When we've been there ten thousand years..." This is a flaw because the song is about being in a timeless place where seconds, hours, years, and decades do not exist. I accept that we do this because we are grappling with the concept of something which is abstract, hard to express with our material framework. Nonetheless, in our quest for spirituality we wrestle with these things and in so doing become sensitive to places of threshold – invitations to move beyond the limits of our body and our mind.

To live a full life with intervals in which we discover the activity of the spirit within us is to increasingly familiarize ourselves with the possibilities of a pause. As we encounter these possibilities, we become more willing to press hold whilst we explore our spirituality. This is like a car journey in which we put aside the schedule as we reach the top of a scenic hill, aiming to enjoy not the road but what is off it. We might pull off to a pleasant café or drive off route to a quaint market town. Yes, it may take longer and may seem a "poor" use of time, but what a difference we notice in the quality of the journey's experience.

My wife and I often count ourselves privileged in life from having survived well and gained a measure of insight from our intense work at St Paul's Centre. Most of our married life had been spent living amongst people we have loved, people who struggled to simply get through the day, who grappled with life on the margins, some with debilitating addictions. The chaos and pain we met daily in our work taught us to appreciate our spirituality and the power of a pause. We learned to intersperse our routines and responsibility with opportunities for the spirit within us to breathe. Giving out emotional and practical support, we came to recognize that our own lives are more than intellect or practical responses, that in making space for our body and brain to rest so too our spirituality should find footing in our lives. At times we stepped back, knowing that when we walked forward again the queue of need would still be there. Against the frailty of our humanity even to the expectation of friends, our resilience remained intact. I believe this was as much the result of moments of pause as it was sleep and nutrition.

To pause became our constant friend. For some years we helped gather food for people in need. There was a steady and manageable flow of donors dropping off food and we were able to chat to them. Those calling to collect the food parcels had appointments sufficiently spaced out to create room for a meaningful encounter with them. We had measured breaks between our encounters with these often interesting and occasionally broken people. In the late 90s we had a less relaxed experience as we responded to an appeal on another continent. Our days went from seeing three or four donors with a few bags of food to hundreds of people and thousands of food bags.

Late one night after a long day of parcelling up aid boxes, the team was exhausted. Everyone looked at the mass of unsorted goods waiting to be processed and collectively knew that it would all still be there in the morning. This was a trigger, a prompting to stop what was clearly important work for a greater importance. Logic dictated that a good night's sleep would return us fresher the following day. Yet there is something other than logic at work in us all, our spirituality, which has a part to play in the renewing and refreshing of our whole being. In some way the pile of work in front of us was one of those triggers, a precious opportunity to stop. We pressed the button, leaving to return in the morning.

The following day it felt a little like we had stopped the film and were now returned to where we left off, but more physically and mentally ready to concentrate. Yet had any of us known in the space between leaving and returning more than our body and mind rested – that the spirit within us had found room to breathe – then we would have known the power of a pause.

You and I build our wisdom and experience around spirituality from those who have walked before us, or from life events, some of which force us to stop. We might look for shortcuts to wisdom, but that rarely brings results. There are few substitutes for spending time listening and being still.

Imagine we are sitting in a memorial service and from out of a quiet reflective moment we hear the following words read out, "There is a time for everything and season for every activity under heaven…" Such words can be a powerful invitation to ponder over what we consider to be important in life. I find funerals to be much like the approaching stroke of midnight on New Year's Eve: they call to something deep inside. These moments seem to fan the desire in us to reevaluate where our priorities are and often we lean towards our sense of spirituality.

Many times I have heard people at funerals say things such as, "I must sit in silence more often, it felt so peaceful. That service felt spiritual I must explore this some time. It is time I learned to meditate," and on and on the declarations sound. Yet as the midnight chime rings out or the last note of the final funeral hymn sounds, the initial mental move towards the invitation to find time for the inner life slowly drains away.

This idea of there being a time for everything is worth exploring. Have you ever noticed how much more comfortable we are with allotting time to what looks like physically productive tasks rather than contemplative tasks? I believe we find commitment to setting aside time to do something like visit a friend or take a sibling for a meal much easier than an abstract commitment like sitting quietly or starting meditation. Society conditions us to see life as a string of doings which more often than not feed into a narrative of productivity. I would argue that there is often missing from the lists of productive doings spirituality – the pursuit of God.

One of the great challenges for many of us is to shift our thinking when it comes to the value of doing vs. being. The value of being when time enters the frame is a prime example. I remember working on a church building project once, and a team member suggested we take a moment to pray at the start of the job each day. We sat in a circle heads bowed and hands fidgeting waiting for someone to say something. Although it felt like an age the wait was short and broken by an elderly chap. He spoke out some thought-provoking words as a prayer. It then went quiet again as his words filled our minds. Then two minutes on and breaking into the calm thought-filled atmosphere a voice said, "Shall we get back to the real stuff now?"

Clearly in the mind of our friend the real stuff or proper work as he saw it included one set of things and excluded another set. Spiritual exercise seemed not to be as valuable as material work or activity, according to his view. The line we read from that poem earlier, which is found in Ecclesiastes, suggesting there is a time for everything, has a list which follows on. Our challenge is not to come to the list limited to the idea that there is valuable or real stuff in life and the not so valuable stuff. My builder friend would be instantly attracted to what the verse describes as a time for building, growing, reaping, or warring. All words in the poem which seem to be a lot about *doing* stuff.

When I read that opening line, "There is a time for everything, and a season for every activity under heaven," I find myself wanting to write next to the word "activity" my own definition. That is not really necessary because the poem includes my list already – a time to sleep, to rest, to gaze out the window thinking nothing in particular and of course placing a pause between any and all those things we think of as the "real" stuff of life.

If we are to discover a deeper spirituality, the power of a pause, then we need to value something not bound by our "doing" mind set.

Over the years we have found so many friends and colleagues exhausted through work. Somehow in the cloud of tiredness, rather than stop, they continue doing what wore them out. Previously they had gained value from giving time to spiritual enrichment. Yet the value and time once placed on regular spiritual exercises is moved to the activities commonly thought of as the real stuff – building, growing, reaping. So focused is our world on tangible result-driven tasks, that resting, sleeping, gazing, or pondering seem not a productive option. Maybe we need to broaden our list of what we value and allow time for *being* as much as we value *doing*! Believe me, whatever "doing" we set aside will all be waiting for us when we come back and press resume. It will not have changed, but we may encounter just as much meaningfulness in the moment we paused.

Stopping on a walk to admire the view is as valuable as the steps we make. I would say taking a moment to stop is not a cessation of the walk but an enhancement to the overall experience along the way. My wife and I were trudging around the Hole of Horcum in the North Yorkshire Moors, England, one year when all of a sudden she stopped. I watched her slowly raise her head and range her eyes across the vast landscape before us. That was over twenty-five years ago, yet I can still hear her words, as fresh and clear today as back then: "This does for my spirit what a good meal does for my stomach." I believe that pausing can do for our spirituality what very few other encounters can. Picking up on that poem and the challenge we have of seeing the value of *being* as well as *doing, we* might say that a walk, like life, is full of rises and falls, steps and stops. Each of these things has value and is part of the overall experience.

Maybe we should say, "There is a time for everything" – "including a pause."

In my early exploration of faith I encountered women and men who seem to have an air of calm. This is of course replicated in many faiths, people who have found space to resist the urge to fill every waking hour with the "real stuff" as our friend in the church maintenance team thought. One dear elderly lady whose home I visited whilst speaking at a church in London gave me a book of her poems. At first I thought, "When will I have time to read this?" Actually she gave me the book to read then and there. We finished our small but adequate meal and remained at the dining table for three hours. She had no TV and the radio was clearly for specific programs. She had adequately filled my stomach and with her poems and silence went on to fill my soul. I found this unusual because in most places where I was a visiting speaker the hosts would want to show me the town or take me bowling or *do* something. This woman saw great value in placing no expectation on me other than to sit, relax, and not even speak.

That night I lay in bed completely relaxed with no sound other than my own internal dialogue. Just as Cheryl had found her soul nourished by the invitation to stop and do nothing other than receive what her eyes fell upon, so I felt my spirit within me inviting me to stop, to pause, to cease my thoughts of doing. I simply experienced *being*. It was the beginning of a long journey towards knowing the sound of my own internal voice and the silence beyond it. It was as though my life had become a film and in pressing pause on as many activities as possible, reducing the incoming messages, I could have a deeper conversation in which even thoughts are not necessary.

To simply rest, be silent, to be contemplative and gaze into space are as valuable as all the constructing, selling, managing, or even film-watching we stuff into our lives.

As I have said elsewhere, the definition of a pause in this book is one in which our whole being is engaged. To pause is to encounter the spirit within us, to move beyond body and mind into our spiritual being. It seems to me that part of the pathway to experience moments of pause is to park some of those things which stimulate our experience of the world of doing stuff. My friend was limited to believing that only construction work is of value because he was blind to that which stimulates or touches on the realm of our spirituality. He, as do we all, needed to practice pressing – seeking out moments of – pause, to make sure there was a "time for everything" not just a limited list of doings. When we favor doing over being we neglect that aspect of ourselves which is the spirit within us.

In response to my thoughts about my grandson pausing the film *Home Alone* to talk with his mum, my friend Ken observed, "It occurs to me that fifty years ago we paused life to watch TV, today we pause TV to do life." I take from my friend's observation that the little button with two lines facilitates the opportunity to come aside from what entertains us to what may enlighten us. That we can put some things on hold for a while and in so doing we might find a richer experience of life.

I find that we need a break from the constant cry of our on-demand world. As we stop the drama unfolding before us, albeit to return to where we left off, we are invited to inhabit the space created with whatever we choose from the list of options in that poem. Will we press pause and create space into which our spirituality may find expression? Or will we be anxious to get back to the film: like my father ignoring his son's questions, will we ignore the voice of the spirit within us?

Pause

Chapter 7

Disconnecting to connect elsewhere

In the film *Mary Poppins* actress Julie Andrews encouraged a whole generation to take medicine with a smile when she sang, "Just a spoonful of sugar helps the medicine go down." It's such an upbeat image and catchy tune that it can obscure a deeper message within. What I found arresting about the storyline is the way in which the father, Mr. Banks, is so serious about life and caught up in work and busyness. It takes quite a bit of disruption to swing his mind round to what he is missing. On the surface of course it appears he is missing out on his children and the experience of fun. Yet as I look a little deeper I see much resistance in my own life to what on the surface appears as purposeless time out.

There are many family films built on the idea of parents struggling to keep it all together, to hold the practicalities of life in balance and be free, joyous and unscripted. In the battle to remain in the game or on top of the game, as some would describe it, there is the need to keep the body healthy, the bank satisfied, and the brain focused. No wonder society churns out loads of Mr. Banks characters who are too serious to take a time-out. So many consider that frivolity.

Here I will add to the mix the challenge of finding time for the spiritual dimension of life. Could it be that time out for such an intangible expression of our existence is a demand too far?

Mr. Banks in the *Mary Poppins* story can't see that his kids want fun not funds. Rather than join them in the park they join him at the bank, with disastrous consequences. Entangled with the practical aspects of life – running a home, managing relationships and tending to finances – he exists in a fog which hides what lies beyond his immediate vision. The hero of the story is Bert, the singing chimney sweep, with no sign of seriousness in him. Bert, aka Dick Van Dyke, catches Mr. Banks off guard with an invitation to walk in the park and fly a kite. Bert guides him to a moment of time-out, of relaxed fun, which opens up a whole new avenue of possibilities for life.

I wonder if from time to time we all need our seriousness broken into by an invitation to leave work and enter the park where we might "go fly a kite, up where the air is light..."

The challenge for Mr. Banks was to disconnect from his own busyness and sense of seriousness about the practical things of his life. None of us wants to be the killjoy who cannot take a bit of time out, yet if it is for something that appears not to advance what we might call the important and tangible things in life, we will resist. When do we find time to enter a space more fitted for, in the case of our thoughts here, less body and mind entanglement in favor of our spiritual nourishment? The hard part is the disconnection with all that we are caught up in! Without that we feel we cannot connect in any other way.

About his decision to become a Jesuit, James Martin SJ writes of the great challenge of letting go of his car, job, and furniture. He concludes that when he arrived at training college with just a couple of suitcases it was in a sense similar to going on holiday. So few were his possessions, he felt liberated from what he had been holding so closely. He writes, "The more we simplify the freer we will feel and be."[12]

There was a time in our own lives when we were firmly embedded in what you might call an all-hands-on-deck experience of life. I was self-employed, and my wife worked during the evening at a nursing home to help get us to the end of the month. This is a common enough picture of a young busy family putting a stake in the ground and throwing everything at it to build a life. Society seems to teach us that being busy and serious, even overworking, is what life is about, what creates success and freedom. Well, we had notions of future independence and freedom somewhere down the line but at that moment all our waking hours were filled. When I think of the image of old Mr. Banks and Bert the chimney sweep dancing in the park holding the string of a kite, I realize there was a time when we had no space to look at the gate of, let alone enter, the park and fly a kite. Perhaps this is your experience? It was ours until a friend concerned for our inner life created a corridor for us to have one of those moments when you become aware that your life consists of more than what you are doing.

Guy, a newly qualified curate, and his wife Tessa came to join the church we were attending. A curate is a new vicar on a test run, and in this one we found a lasting friend. He turned out to be kind and faithful, a great addition to the community. We were a city familiar with a number of social challenges; not least unemployment and the social and relational stress that that brings. We guessed this encounter with people in social, emotional and relational poverty contrasted with Guy's own journey, one blessed with the love of a family, a good education, and a well-paid job. All of which, and it's refreshing to say, made him a compassionate and tenacious advocate for others. On a spiritual level he emitted a deep sense of otherworldliness, something more than kindness or religious speech. Over time we learned that he tackled life much like the founder of his faith, creating space for others to live beyond the confines of sight – to "walk by faith," as one ancient text reads. One of my builder friends, on meeting Guy, commented, "He's a proper gent," and he is.

One evening we heard a knock on our front door. It was Guy, so we invited him inside. Cheryl was getting ready for a night shift at a local nursing home and I was still in my hairy builder's gear – dusty jeans and dirty hands. Guy talked about creating space in the demands of our busy life and the need for what that busyness couldn't nurture or nourish. He talked about a cottage he knew of that we could retreat to. It was in a rural village surrounded by trees, hills, and farmland. He was proposing we take some time out where there was less distraction and an opportunity to experience some silence and solitude. This was a place he would ensure we had all we needed and the room to find some refreshment for our soul.

We wanted to go but it was out of the question, we were too busy and too tired to stop, too connected to disconnect. I wonder how many of us wake up one morning and just know that all our energy and drive is too heavily invested in one area of our life and that another dimension exists but we just can't get to it? That was us. It wasn't a holiday Guy was suggesting, a thrill adventure and cultural experience. It was a space to invest in our spirit, our spirituality, our inner being.

It's not easy or seemingly practical, especially when the budget is tight and living is demanding, to step back. Taking time to be disconnected from it all is low on the agenda when we are entangled in and negotiating our way through the complexities of living. For many of us, putting an interval in the drama of our lives can be just another problem to solve or a task to squeeze in, as we found.

James Martin writes of the need for silence or separation from the busyness and noise of life. He suggests one reason we shy away from taking time out is that "we fear we might hear from the deepest part of ourselves." I believe this is the spirit within us. Martin also makes the point that, "You cannot change our noisy world, but you can disconnect from time to time."[13]

It was 1988 and I was newly self-employed so we had no room for rest or retreats in our thinking or conversation. Do you ever feel like that, when it's impossible to imagine disconnecting, even for a short while? We still have an old freezer which is not frost-free. This means left to its own devices it gets iced up and sometimes the door won't shut properly. As it gets worse we think to ourselves we'll defrost it before we next go shopping. That means unplugging it and letting the ice slowly melt – it's therapeutic to watch if we have the time! But of course we don't find the time, we don't unplug it, and the ice continues to grow. Inevitably we arrive back from the supermarket with frozen food and can't fit it in. Now we have to defrost quickly with scrapers and hot water which produce broken lumps of ice – we get water everywhere. Obviously the freezer has more room afterwards, but the whole process is fraught and unnecessary.

It seems there is never a right moment to pull the plug. We always seem to put off taking time out because other things are more important, more urgent, and maybe more fulfilling emotionally.

When our friend Guy made the offer to help us with taking some time out at the cottage, we had two young daughters taking most of our energy, a house soaking up all our income, and work stretching out decades ahead of us. In short we had excuses. I can still find excuses thirty-five years on. The excuses I use now are different, but they come from the same misreading of life at a spiritual as well as emotional and physiological level.

Buried beneath our busyness in life, Cheryl and I had a desire to nurture and develop a meaningful spirituality. I find this not uncommon, that people have a desire for spirituality, but it seems too distant or unreachable. Spirituality can easily take a back seat when more tangible and obvious stuff needs to be done. We also found it hard to articulate what we desired spiritually. Yet Guy seemed to tune in to this questioning within us. He saw that we had no room to oxygenate the vessels which might bring life to the spirit within.

In past chapters we have explored how there is little room for doubt that we are more than our physical bodies and complex thoughts, that we have another dimension to our being. Yet we are mostly caught up with sustaining what we might describe as those two obvious thirds of our being, the body and mind. Yet whatever we name it, spirit, soul or true self, we at least recognize the presence of what we might know as an interior life or existence beyond our framework of normal language. When I think about this inner me, the spirit within, I mean to articulate more than psychology or emotional responses from my brain waves. What I term as "the spirit within" is not nourished or stimulated with fish and chips, music or travel, but with silence, solitude, and space. There can be a busy connectedness: "I like to keep busy," says a friend who argues that in her busyness she is most content. Yet when we talk some more, it becomes clear the busyness does nothing to create a noiseless seclusion in which to dwell spiritually.

It is as though we have an unrecognizable hunger, a thirst for a drink we can't quite identify. A teenager may say she doesn't feel right. The mother will ask, have you eaten, did you sleep last night, has something happened at college? She is working through categories which may help to identify the problem. But what if we don't have an obvious category? What if we have a spiritual hunger and only apply the questions from the categories of the mind or body?

F.C. Happold, in his book *Mysticism*, speaks of the great challenge there is in understanding the mystic. This is because mystics see or experience a world "beyond, of something which, though it is interwoven with it, is not of the external world of material phenomena."[14] No matter how we frame our questions, the mystic's experience is from a category outside those we use.

Our challenge is to first recognize the importance of the other third – the spirit within us. It is from here, not the recesses of memory and longings of emotion, where the spirit's quiet voice speaks. Not in audible words or complex thoughts, not in a rumbling tummy or aching back, yet still as clear if we can find a way to tune into the realm of spirituality. In a way unique to the spiritual realm, the spirit within us says, "Don't forget me."

Along with you, I am on this journey of discovery and long to be able to lay out the alphabet of spiritual language – but I can't. We are here grappling with the nature of an abstract reality. This is much like the question someone may ask of us, "Show me God?" In our response we may use images that stir the emotions or language that stimulates intellectual intrigue. I wonder if we might better serve the questioner by directing them to the spirit within as their true voice of enquiry after God.

Bede Griffiths retells the story of a fellow Benedictine monk living in South India, Fr. Jules Monchanin. One day Fr. Jules approached a group of schoolchildren and asked them, "Where is God?"[15] The Christian children pointed upward to heaven but the Hindu children pointed to the heart and said that God was there. Griffiths points out in his writing that we can be confused with where God is and where we are as spiritual beings. In India he often met with people asking, "Who am I? Am I this body sitting here? Am I this personality relating to other people? Or is there something deeper within, beyond my body and my mind? Is there a deeper reality in me?"

I want to say yes, and it is this *spiritual* reality which seeks to connect with God and it is this *spiritual* reality which we encounter when we enter a pause.

You may know the whisper of an inner voice which longs for us to put a space between the flows of our activity. That voice, as it were, wants to be a priority in the same way eating and sleeping are. If we don't eat or sleep, we become dysfunctional, unable to process or even stay coherent. Think about the great depths of comfort and assurance emotionally we derive from relationships, which if neglected leave us feeling lost and lonely. The more I explore and reach into the realm of my own spirituality, the more I realize that to neglect this area of my life is not dissimilar to that of neglecting the other areas – the consequences of which are dysfunction and ultimately a poverty of existence. There is of course no guarantee that we will, given the opportunity, reprioritize our focus even for a brief moment in time. The great challenge as we have found is not to know we are more than our work and words, more than flesh and blood, houses and activity, but to disconnect a little from these things to connect with our spirit within.

I get that it can be simple to say and complex to execute when we become aware that time-out is as important as time-in. Take the advent of social media and all that hangs around it: this has greatly removed our time alone and the principle of being off-duty. Not new but on the rise is the notion of home-working. "The butcher, baker, and candlestick maker," is a phrase that reflects a history before the industrial era. In such a period and for many people working from home was because they lived above the workshop. It had its downside and some benefits, but overall, when the closed sign was out, so was the work disruption. The ovens were cold, the wax solid, the meat put in the store.

That is vastly different to what is now working from home because there is the creeping connectedness of social media, e-mail, text, Twitter, and so on. Workloads and working time can become blurred. We are connected all the time, and time spent is less important than tasks completed. Most of us struggle to disconnect, we log off a system but periodically glance at the e-mail icon on our phone. It's not easy to stop. You see, the really tricky thing to manage is the seeming importance of the voice from the two-thirds shouting, "Me first." Trying to slow it down or squeeze a space for spiritual breath in there is hard. Over an evening meal we glance at our phone, see the subject line in an e-mail, and think we'll just open it and look with one eye. There goes the next hour.

Back in the 1980s Cheryl and I were wrestling with the idea of stopping our day-to-day dash and its distraction from the needs of our spirit, our spirituality in life. The challenge was to recognize there is more to our existence than what occupied, even at times possessed us! Yet to think of disconnecting brought us worry, we were anxious about work and the cost of what sounded like going to the middle of nowhere to do nothing.

Sadly it hit all those "it's not a productive use of time" thoughts we have been tricked into thinking by corporate management. Subtly we are looking for a return on investment – what will I get if I stop doing the thing that feeds my body and mind and give space to my spirit? There is also the thought that *we* are the center of all that happens. I have known many times when I have put off a retreat opportunity because I think things will fall apart without me. This thinking had paid my grandiose ego dividends.

Some of us have given much thought to the need to create space for reflection, balance, and emotional resilience. Again, we have the desire. The bookshelves of many reveal a hunt for that magic help-me-to-let-go formula. They are mostly aimed at taking control, at managing your life. All helpful information, but I wonder if even with the structure of our day-to-day lives being under control it actually nurtures the spirit within us.

Who of us hasn't had time in both camps? In one camp, all in the garden is in order and we have no rush or panic – life is tidy. Of course, we've spent a lot of time tending the garden. In the other camp, we walk through life in disarray, driven by every demand and voice. I think of the second line of *Proud Mary* in the Creedence Clearwater Revival song: "Working for the man every night and day... big wheels keep on turning." At times it feels like they will never stop. But does either camp bring us into the spiritual life?

Mr. Banks was firmly connected to living in only two of those thirds I spoke of earlier, the body and mind. He invested in what he perceived he believed to be *real life*. His was a struggle, as many of us know, to connect with the value of time away from his perceived productive activities. On a spiritual level this is where sadly our focus is on the stimulation our body and mind enjoy and not the spirit within us.

What Cheryl and I discovered was that we can express life beyond the walls of, as one first century-writer says, "The tent in which we live."

John of the Cross, a man who spent considerable time in a small cell, spoke of this tent as a "household" with three parts. When two were at rest, namely the body and mind, he was able to exercise the life of the spirit within him. As he reflected in his poem the *Dark Night of the Soul*, John said that the "lower operations of his household" were at war with his spirituality. He describes wrestling with what he termed, "The enemies." He says the control those two-thirds have over our whole being, "Hinder the soul from attaining the supernatural blessing of the union of love of God, for whilst these are alive and active, this cannot be…"[16]

For us to connect with this inner being, the spirit within us, we need to find a space in which to disconnect from the demands of the body and mind.

We limit our investment in our spirituality by not taking time out, creating room for the spirit within us.

After twenty years of working without a significant break, not entirely but partly through a sense that to let go would be to lose my spot, I paused for some months. I learned that stuff was still there when I returned, that the world hadn't collapsed half as quickly as I thought it might. The real lesson I came away with is not the consequence to my work from putting it down but of the opportunity lost by not picking up on my spirituality.

In time it was to our benefit that we listened out for the many *Berts* in life who came along with a smile and said, "What you need, governor, is a walk in the park and to fly a kite." Many of us come to recognize that we very rarely see what we need in ourselves. I'm guessing you know this, that however competent and self-aware we become there is always room for a nudge where we are blind to a need, room for Guy and a cottage.

When our friend Guy suggested creating space to invest in our spirit, our spirituality, our inner being, there was no breath between that and the offer of the cottage. Thirty-five years on and we have never forgotten the wisdom and kindness of what

Guy did. It was like those occasions we all have of seeing food on the cheek of a friend. Do we point it out, do we ignore it? The best thing is probably to offer a napkin and direct them to consider a specific spot on their chin. Guy was simply saying, "Have you thought of some quiet and solitude? I know where you can find it."

In fact what he actually did was amazing.

As Cheryl and I considered accepting the offer that Guy had made, our minds eased into the usual objections. We had little money, the children were young, and we only had my builder's van to travel in. Gently and without challenging pressure, Guy came back at us with, "If those excuses were removed would you take the offer of some time out?" So often we see a barrier which obscures the bridge standing next to it. Perhaps we fear less what we are letting go of than the spiritual mystery we may be picking up.

That is the core of it for us all; clearing the room to do something is not the same as doing it. Disconnecting from the body and mind entanglements sometimes comes before we find a space of solitude, silence, and spiritual nourishment. The day we left for the cottage Guy hired a car for us, gave us a map and directions. On our arrival a near neighbour to the remote cottage had filled the fridge. All excuses were now taken away along with the noise or knocks on the door. All that remained was to oxygenate our spiritual lungs. This became a pattern, not cottages and seclusion, but some equity of investment in all three dimensions of our being, body, and mind – and of course the spirit within us.

Imagine what it was like for Mr. Banks with all that important stuff to do or Proud Mary with her good job in the city working every night and day? Yes, they are fictional characters who were making changes to invest in feeling better. In them we see a refocusing of attention away from what had become the main event in their lives, money and position. From them I learn that disconnecting does not come without some disruption. I wonder what difference it would make if we thought less of the challenge of disconnecting and more of the benefit of connecting to the spirit within us.

Whilst at the cottage all those years ago we discovered the void that the space created was easily filled with long moments of meditation, sitting with little to do but the opportunity to just *be*. Yes, our body was rested and our minds in less need of complex or worrisome activity. In part, I suspect we were like John of the Cross sitting in his cell – set free to receive the love of his God to know life is more than being busy about our work. To say how it felt to spend time alone with our spirit is a challenge because such moments are not feelings-based as we would understand feelings. They were moments where there was an absence of conflict or competition between each of those thirds which make us whole – like the third child in a family photoshoot, elbowing through to be in the center for once.

What of us? How caught up in feeding the body and stimulating the mind are we? I wonder if you too have a quiet voice, your spirit within saying, "Leave some room for me?"

Pause

Chapter 8

Nature's spiritual voice

One Friday afternoon during coffee with a friend, he teased me about the column I had submitted that week to our local newspaper. He was amused not so much by what I wrote but by the position on the page where the editor always placed the weekly thoughts. The "Christian Comment," for design reasons, was placed amongst the notices of the dead. My friend commented that he saw my name in the obituary column, adding, "Once again!"

Obviously there will come a time when my family *will* put my name in the obituaries announcing that I died and the funeral will be held on some particular date. Until then, my appearances on the obituary pages will remain due not to death but the unfortunate layout of the column I contributed to.

Those weekly thoughts I wrote were short and took little time to read. In some ways they were a mini version of the BBC Radio 2 program *Pause for Thought*, in which the presenter would often pose a philosophical question or idea. In the week that my friend made his joke with me, I had written a thought based on an interesting experience I had had that summer.

Unplanned and with a measure of stress, I had taken to resting on a wonderfully knobbly oak tree. It was one of those days when I needed to not be me, to be absent from the revolving thoughts in my head. It was one of those days when a member of my team had pushed and pressed me for an answer to a question I could not give at that time.

We have all experienced being pressured by someone asking for something we don't have the capacity to give. These can be particularly painful and embarrassing moments which can carry a pressure too much to bear. There are moments when we just can't respond the way others want us to. We can find ourselves trapped between no response and a wrong response. Many times I have known that to say "I don't know the answer" is a perfectly good response next to the alternative, which is exactly what my interrogator doesn't want to hear.

So having been cornered and pressed to the point of bursting, I decided on this occasion it seemed good to do the flight thing before I had a dual appearance in the local newspaper: "Reverend Breaks Nose of Charity Worker in Fight over Volunteer Hours. See his spiritual comment *How to forgive* on this week's obituary page!"

Flight on this occasion meant taking refuge under an oak tree, the trunk of which resembled something out of the *BFG* movie. It felt good. There is something solid and dependable even timeless about contact with a part of creation, a part which has and will outlive you. It does us good to acknowledge that the natural world invariably gives rather than takes from us humans. The warm sun and not intolerable lack of breeze eased my mind, allowing tension to leak from me as the air does from a slow puncture on a cycle wheel. For a while it seemed all my troubled and anxious thoughts had left me. Obviously this was not permanent!

I suspect it is impossible to stop thinking. Yet our conscious and unconscious thoughts have a massive impact on all kinds of aspects of our lives. Many people suffer from stress-related symptoms even when they have no sense of being stressed. Headaches, stomach upsets, and mood swings all feel so physical that a person can assume there must be something physically wrong. Yet it is not until the doctor asks, "Is something bothering you?" and the patient says, "Come to think of it, Doctor..." and then the jumbled thoughts come tumbling out, revealing the reason for the sleepless nights, the lack of interest in food or those fight-and-flight feelings. In many instances a doctor may prescribe medication to relax or calm a person but not to stop thought processes altogether.

It may well be a neurological impossibility for our brain to stop all thought, but I understand that in a meditative state we move away from the influence of our thoughts. This is in part what happened to me under the tree that day.

I can't say for certain that this was the very first time I truly experienced meditation, but it was an amazing introduction to the wonderful part that the natural world can play in helping us access a deeper spiritual experience, and one which is beyond the world of our thoughts.

As I lay with my eyes closed under that old oak tree (no yellow ribbon in sight), I tuned into the sound of a song thrush. More than simple entertainment for my ears, along with the feel of the tree on my back I was drawn into a profound meditation which touched the inner me, the spirit within me. Perhaps you have wondered at some time what role a bird or tree, star, or mountain has in our spiritual life? Without seeking or wanting this sense of connection, I came upon an experience that felt like my spirit and the natural world were caught up in a single moment of existence, like lovers entwined. It was for minutes not hours – certainly not the forty-nine days Buddha spent under his tree! Of course Jesus is reported to have ended his forty days in the wilderness whilst being attended to by animals. I'm guessing there was a bird or two around.

Working to understand and articulate how this meditation took place meant that I needed to think differently after the event. My views of the human relationship to all creation moved, and as a result I have begun to explore the possibility of an intimacy with nature I had previously not considered.

I wonder if we all have fixed points of reference which need to be challenged to enable a reevaluation of our understanding of the power and place of nature in our spiritual lives. The felt strength of an oak and the smooth voice of a song thrush to some might be described as God speaking through or out of the voice of nature. Over time I have become more comfortable with the idea that the whole of creation has a part to play in all aspects of the body, mind, and the spirit within us. I would of course on this occasion return to the office for that difficult conversation with the awkward team member. Yet during that time under the tree no thought of the staff encounter had influence over me – neither it nor the conversation I would have back at the office in the future existed in my consciousness.

It was a moment of pause.

As I said earlier, if we could stop thinking, or at least stop the thoughts that trouble us, we might find a deeper rest, this place of pause. You and I know that much of the mental and emotional turmoil we face can exert influence over, if not actually form, our thoughts, thoughts of what has happened or might happen rather than the bare facts of what is. Yet there is the space in-between wherein we might pause. I'm not suggesting meditation or leaning on a tree as a form of planned therapy, though it might be; rather more that they are mechanisms for suspending the influence of our thoughts on our present experience of life.

This phrase I use, *the in-between place*, is one which reminds me that to pause is to lose the grip that time and knowledge has on me. Let me explain.

Our thoughts, we are told by scientists and psychologists, are a product of the information in our brain. We have a bank of memories we call upon to inform our present and form a view of the future. In his book *The Order of Time*, Carlo Rovelli writes of time as a marker for changing events. He suggests from a philosophical stance that there is only one unit of time and that is the present into which we draw on that bank of *past* memories. We also create a future through projecting what knowledge or memories we have into imagined future events. Rovelli reflects on the question Aristotle asked, "What is time?" and the answer which comes back is, "If nothing changes, then time does not pass."[17] In the quest for moments of pause, I have come to recognize that this in-between place is in some way a halting of the information transfer from memories to projections.

Many of us are familiar with the words of Psalm 23 about the shepherd and the green pastures with cool still water – an idyllic scene. Whenever I read it I want to be there, to lose myself as I wander along those still quiet waters, but mostly because it says my soul will be refreshed. That's gotta be more than easing a troubled mind – that's about the inner you, the deepest part of yourself being refreshed. When we think of being refreshed, often we imagine being hot and having a cold drink, being tired and having a good sleep. The drink and the sleep are the in-between bit: tired – *sleep* – refreshed.

Could it be, I wonder, if there is a role here for the tree, the bird, and the stars in certain circumstances to be the in-between bit? The voice of a bird, the power of the wind and yes, crazy as it sounds, the feel of a tree. These are in some ways an unadulterated voice, the voice placed in them through their creator without the bias of human intervention or engineering.

Even writing these things makes me uncomfortable. I want to unpack it all and tell you what I *don't* mean by voice in a tree. In short, I can say we don't make sleep or a cold glass of water a god by recognizing they played a part in refreshing our physical body. Neither is there a need to fear making a deity of these other things which clearly help to refresh our spirit.

Captivated by the sky above and no doubt tucked in a desert watching sheep, the Psalmist David spoke of the infinite expanse of the universe. It intrigues me that he wrote of the stars, "Day after day they pour forth speech; night after night they reveal knowledge. They have no speech as we understand spoken language, they use no words; no sound is heard from them. Yet their voice goes out into all the earth, their words to the ends of the world."

The nineteenth-century poet Longfellow looked into the same night sky and wrote his poem "The Light of Stars." Of the planet

Mars he says it's a "star of strength," and he is changed, his mood is altered by his encounter. "I see thee stand, And smile upon my pain." Longfellow speaks of the stars reaching down towards him and increasing his strength, reducing his pain.

In the second century an early Christian scholar named Origen wrote, "I think that God who made all things in wisdom so created all the species of visible things upon earth, that he placed in them some teaching and knowledge of things invisible…"[18] Origen seemed to suggest that there is an invisible world, existence, or power which can be known or experienced through the visible expression of nature.

On that bright sunny day with my body propped against the tree, sitting under the canopy of the oak with a song thrush perched to share its message, I moved imperceptibly to a soul-refreshing moment. I moved from conscious awareness of my body and mind to the spirit within me. A voice, a language I did not know nor needed to know, touched me in the way David and Longfellow had been touched. Such a voice transported me beyond my thoughts and to the ending of any influence they had on my experience of life at that moment. This is a moment of pause, a spiritual walk along the banks of a crystal-clear river, a gaze into the majestic night sky where the full impact of all creation, not just the bit we have taken control over, intertwines with the inner us.

As I share the story of my experience under the tree, my hope is that you too will pick up the challenge of inviting the natural world, not so much to speak but to help you to stop speaking. The power of our thinking over our experience of life can be of great deflection from our spirituality, yet to stop thinking is too unimaginable, maybe even scientifically not possible, but to put a pause in those thoughts makes a difference. Evelyn Underhill describes such moments as, "Where the self is released from succession, the voices of the world are never heard, and the great adventure of the spirit takes place."

The Italian friar Saint Francis of Assisi was a bit of a Dr. Doolittle in terms of communicating with animals. We might be able to see the attraction if we have had to deal with difficult humans for long enough! Ugolino Brunforte wrote *The Little Flowers of St. Francis* in which there are animal tales. In one such tale Francis spoke about God to a flock of birds that remained on a tree listening to him. On another occasion he had a two-way conversation with a wolf. Although a devoted believer in God as the creator not the created, Francis saw no conflict with connecting to God through and in nature. Bonaventure says, "Francis was filled with great affection for all creatures because he realised that we all come from the same creative source in God."[19]

Always in plain sight, our true surroundings are not the structures we build but the natural world we have been gifted with. Many of us have found companionship, comfort, and character in pets. In our house we debate whether or not our pets will be in the life beyond our current sight. I confess two of our dogs would get my vote. When alone in the house with Barnie, a big hairy Newfoundland, I would talk to him, nothing too deep, and he would give me a look that said, "I have no idea what you're saying but I appreciate being consulted." I do not need to be an animist to recognize that my living breathing dog had a greater role to play in my life than fetching a ball or biting a burglar.

I find no real spiritual conflict in the animal stories, or talking to the dog, rhetorical questions to the night sky, other than this question: does this connection to or with the nonhuman world indicate that such elements of creation have a role in our own spiritual development or diet? Clearly it did in the spiritual life of Francis, which in the end is marked by his well-known profound meditation and prayer. You can look it up, but here is the lead in: "Make me an instrument of your peace." Each line is a desire to be on the other side of the things that greatly trouble us, hatred, doubt, despair, sadness, and so on. Is it possible that Francis discovered in the natural world an opportunity to still his mind and dwell in the present, that any expression of hatred, doubt, fear, or despair in him found less influence on his life than the natural world?

During life, we may also find an invitation to pause prompted by nature. At times when we are able to recognize that our negative thoughts have taken our life experience captive, an option might be to look to the rest of creation. Often, simply placing yourself in the path of the natural world to lean into its vastness and might can move your spirituality from despair and sadness to joy and hope. The bit that interests me, the part that I am opening up for your consideration, is the bit in-between our thoughts holding us captive and nature setting us free. Whilst there is great value in replacing one set of thoughts for another, I believe the kind of moment or meditation that can help transform our experience of life is not to pause for thought but to pause *from* thoughts.

Following the pause under that tree one late September, I wrote in my diary, "A quiet refreshing distance seems to exist between me and the harsh reality of the world around me. I returned knowing an increased resilience had entered me like a newly charged battery." I was surprised by my own lack of interest during this pause in any solution to what worried me. The problem remained but I had changed. It would be great to tell you this lasted for hours and brought about a profound insight and endless spiritual depth. In truth it lasted twenty minutes after which the bark hurt my back and a passing motorist, by the volume of his radio, had forgotten his hearing aids!

The power of a pause can be found in our response to the invitation of nature to dwell and receive from it. The audible sound of a bird and mighty presence of a tree may be a voice which the spirit within us alone can resonate with. We may have only seconds, minutes, hours, or days before the next life encounter interrupts the space where no other apart from our God can intrude. There is an inexplicable calming intimacy available to us when we listen to the voice of nature, a voice we hear with our spirit and not our mind.

Pause

Chapter 9

The voice of the spirit within us

Boiled cabbage and gravy smells drifted over us as the meals were being served on the ward. Bob, our mandolinist, was nowhere to be seen as the food trolley rattled and neared our audience, the patients on ward four at our city's main hospital. It was Christmas and our small music group was about to sing carols, ahead of the evening meal round.

Bob finally arrived and immediately knelt to open his case. Bending to his ear, I said, "Bob, Bob, what's the problem, mate? We need you now." His shoulders were shaking, and I thought he was crying, upset by something. I asked in a soft voice if everything was okay.

Had I gotten a little closer to Bob's ear I would have smelt the reason for his lateness and odd behavior. He'd had a glass or two of wine at his office Christmas party which had reduced Bob to a giggling wreck. For reasons only he could know Bob had found something amusing at the sight of bandages and bedpans. We began the set, a list of familiar Christmas carols, and he eventually joined in averting his eyes from his wife who was unimpressed.

Bob, an Anglican married to a Catholic, played in our eclectic music group in which I, who had no musical gifts, was stuck on the bongos! We were all looking for some kind of spiritual experience that had an element of fun. On some level Bob and I were worlds apart. I was a builder, he was a professional in a legal firm. He wore suits and earned his money with a pen and clever words. I wore jeans, had a pencil behind my ear, and whistled a lot. Yet we found common ground, a sense of fun together.

For some time Bob had wanted to expand or at least explore his spirituality through a traditional-style pilgrimage. He saw in this the opportunity to push himself both physically, through the walking, and spiritually through reflection at the shrine or whatever he arrived at. Yes, you guessed it, I joined him.

In life many of us sense an inner calling to seek spirituality. There is a voice that is more than mental curiosity, a voice whose origin is the spirit within us. In this chapter I want us to explore what responding to this voice meant for Bob and me on one particular occasion. How in a way we were led to take a brief time away from home and work life whilst we went in pursuit of spirituality. The challenge, as you will read, was to not see this as a single event simply kicked off by an inner voice to which we might later become unresponsive as we journeyed.

So, one night over a shared meal the subject of a pilgrimage came up. Bob really fancied the experience of a long walk and had the idea that the physical exertion was connected with an inner voice calling for the development or creation of a new insight into his spirituality. I liked the thought of an adventure and had a stirring in me to expand my own faith in a way I could not articulate. By the time dessert was served, I was almost on board. Over coffee, Bob's wife encouraged me to join him. She was quite insistent as I recall.

Not since his Boy Scout days had Bob done any real hiking. I was the same. We knew some preparation was needed. We gave some thought and planning to this and Bob began by leaving the car and walking to the train station for his commute to work. I figured running up and down ladders with my work was near enough. Looking back, hindsight being a wonderful thing, we should have done more preparation both physically and spiritually in advance of our adventure.

To test our mettle before we set off on the big adventure we walked part of the Black Mountains. These are found in Wales near the Brecon Beacons National Park, a popular walking and climbing area. Our confidence took somewhat of a knock when at the top of Hay Bluff along a part of Offa's Dyke Path, which borders England and Wales, we couldn't work out which direction to go. Our map skills were weak and we encountered a valuable lesson, pause before you plough on.

First walking in one direction, we then changed our mind and came back to where we started. As I recall we got confused about whether to turn the compass or the map; locating ourselves on the map was proving difficult. Whatever Bob had learned in his Boy Scout days had long leaked from his mind. Had we stopped thinking about the destination, maps, and compasses, had we taken a moment out and paused, we may have returned with clearer vision. We didn't!

Near where we stood, the bracken moved, followed by a voice, "You lads lost?" Sadly it wasn't a Moses' moment, no fire in the bush. We tried to sound confident, but we weakened as we realized the bushes were shielding a group of soldiers on exercise. This explained the markings on the map – MOD. We had strayed near some Ministry of Defence land with soldiers on military exercises.

The day didn't get any better and culminated in us coming down the wrong side of a mountain, miles from where we had planned. A five-mile walk took us to the nearest village and phone box. Our wives repatriated us back to the cottage. This was a pattern to be repeated!

From Coventry to Glastonbury. It all felt epic with 120 miles by foot ahead of us.

On the morning of our departure one of our friends, a local vicar, came and prayed for us, adding to the sense of anticipation. Great things were ahead – inner peace, divine glow, spiritual significance. This was a pause from our normal life, time off work and away from family and home. For the next few days, Bob and I would stop being a legal administrator and builder to become seekers of enlightenment. It was my goal to put an end to my smoking habit, something I had found difficult. Symbolically, I took no cigarettes with me and intended that was the end of it – I was bargaining with God! Best laid plans and all!

People from all over the world walk ancient routes and pathways to and from places of spiritual and historical interest. Whether a stone building or mound of earth has inherent power to influence our inner spirituality is hard to say. Yet the knowledge of past events, the insight from our internal dialogue en route and the presence of others pausing their normal daily life as they travel the same path heightens our sense of hope. Hope that we might be changed or at least encounter a spirituality that is refreshing to our inner being.

So here we were, bravely walking away from all that security and comfort, love and care, into the unknown. We had pressed pause on normal life in the hope of a richer depth to our spirituality. Blessed by our vicar friend and fortified with a better set of directions, we settled into our stride towards Glastonbury.

Sometime around mid-morning we realized it was hot. We didn't know until later that night it was nearing the hottest day on record for that time of year, July. One road we walked on was being resurfaced with tarmacadam, and it felt like walking over hot coals. But we pressed on – Glastonbury in our sights.

The site of both the first Christian church in England and a mecca for Druids, Glastonbury is a place of mystery and mysticism. Attracting Christians from around the world is the legendary story of Joseph of Arimathea. Apart from being the man who took control of the burial of Jesus, he supposedly brought Jesus as a young man on a visit when trading in the area. Some believe that Joseph returned after the crucifixion with the Holy Grail, a wooden cup used at the last supper. It's not a very credible story nor accepted by historians, but it sells a lot of hotel rooms for the night!

William Blake in the 1800s added to the momentum of this narrative in his poem which is now a famous hymn, "And did those feet in ancient time, Walk upon England's mountains green: And was the holy Lamb of God, On England's pleasant pastures seen!" If the thought of standing on turf that Jesus stood on is not enough, there is also the legend of King Arthur and that of Glastonbury Abbey being his last resting place. Wow, there really is something for everyone!

My friend Bob was more interested in these legends and myths than I. In many ways we had arrived at our own points of faith from different starting places and neither of us were finished in our search for spirituality. That said, Glastonbury as a place of spiritual interest was not on my radar. The pathway of faith and spirituality down which I had so far walked did not include ancient sites and religious history.

Faith and spirituality in my life at that time was an individual and private matter, between me and God. I was a nonconformist, just as my school reports had prophesied! Lighting candles in my world was done because the money in the electricity meter had run out or there was a general strike. Nonreligious was the flavor of my first twenty-two years, although at this point I had encountered faith and "all that stuff." The churches I had first attended were plain and without religious furniture, bland and void of a sense of history. The idea of 120 miles of walking was fine, but to find meaning in a sacred shrine or holy place was for weird New Age folk or Catholics, not me.

Twenty miles from home a subtle voice inside me suggested I remove my boots and socks to dip my hot, sore, and smelly feet into a nearby river. It was invigorating. Noticing Bob had some discomfort in one foot, I encouraged him to follow suit. He declined and said he would wait till the end of the day. I could tell that it was a problem. I suspect he too had an inner voice nudging him to take off his boots. Here was one of those take-a-moment-out-and-pause opportunities not entered! Mile followed mile, and the heat was getting to us as we passed through small villages and hamlets. Our route took us on long roads which stretched out endlessly before us.

The urge to keep going is strong in many of us. Our everyday lives can be filled with energy and fun but peppered with moments of stress and distraction from our spirituality. For Bob and me this walk was a way of focusing on our spirituality in a way our everyday lives seems not to allow. How often have I thought, "I'll just keep going until..." That sign post, milestone, or date in the future seems to get further away, and the journey can feel longer. Yet we press on. Bob's words at that riverbank, "I'll wait till the end of the day," have served as a reminder to not wait. So often there is a voice saying loosen your laces, dangle your feet in the river, rest, and we respond with, "I'll wait till..."

It was approaching evening when we neared Moreton-in-Marsh on a Roman road leading into the town where we intended to stay that first night. Four hours after the river break and knowing we were on the final push of the day, we rested. Bob braved it and took off his boots. I was glad because my knee was beginning to hurt. What must we have looked like, limping along and hiding our pain from each other, both no doubt questioning whether we could make it.

Peeling off his boot and sock Bob revealed what I at first thought was a plastic bag filled with water. Never before or since have I seen such a blister. I thought to myself, why is he wearing a plastic bag under his sock? On closer inspection it was not a plastic bag, it was the skin on the whole of his heel filled with water. The biggest blister you could imagine was hanging there, off his foot. He popped it, and the relief was short-lived. Bob's face said it all, this was painful; how much further could he go?

We rang Bob's wife from a phone box in Moreton-in-Marsh. After walking thirty-seven miles, we made it no further. It was a bit of a déjà vu moment, as not many weeks earlier on our ill-fated training walk in the Black Mountains we had called in our wives to rescue us then.

Whilst we waited for Bob's wife, I walked into an off-license (liquor store) and bought a packet of cigarettes. I enjoyed that smoke, but it was another goal unmet.

It felt good to know that later that night I would sleep in my own bed and not a bush. We both felt terrible and regretful, yet it had been an adventure. With his foot and my knee, we had unnecessary excuses to call it off.

We never did walk to Glastonbury, but we never forgot that day.

Looking back, I can see how comfortable it felt to view our time away from home and work as an event or goal, something to be executed. It seems so natural to hear a call, the voice of the spirit within, pointing towards a cathedral down the road and then to set off in pursuit. Why would we not want to get to and be in the place we had perceived we were directed to? Why would we not wish to press on towards a well of wisdom from which to drink?

Yet such thinking is flawed in that our spirituality is inextricably linked to the spirit within us. Our desire to explore spirituality is more than an influence by our inner spirit, it is the exposure of the spirit within us as part of our whole being. In seeing our journey as a place to be reached, the moving of our body and mind towards, say, a pilgrimage site, we stopped listening to the ever present spirit within us in each step we took towards the destination.

It just so happens my wife is a brilliant navigator and when we travel together with me driving, something strange happens. My navigation system just parks itself. I take no notice of where we are, and I don't even read road signs, as I enjoy the scenery. We talk and we listen to each other, we tune into the voice of the other. There are moments when we have conflict but not often.

Now, when I take a trip on my own in the car, Cheryl often waves me off and checks if I have the map or I know where I'm going. Then I promise, "I'll ring when I get there." Once I leave, I don't expect to hear her speak, so I don't listen for her voice.

I wonder sometimes if we tune out of the voice that calls us to pause because we are so used to travelling alone.

As I reflect on how Bob and I approached our trip, it was in some way with hope for increased spirituality at the destination, not on the journey. We tuned out of the voice of the spirit within us because we had not considered or expected to hear that voice until we arrived at our destination.

I have no doubt that the same voice which influenced both of us to seek a deeper spirituality, to put aside our work and home life for a time, was the same voice that also whispered along the route to pause. This same voice calls us to moments of pause along the path of life, not simply at milestones or monuments.

What might it mean for you to step out of the line for a while and walk a different path, holding a spiritual hope or expectation as you go? Walking is of course exchangeable here with almost any pursuit that is not the norm. The pause was not and could not be the experience of exchanging one set of activities, working and home life, for another, walking. The pause I learned of was to continue to listen and not stop listening to the first call to seek a deeper spirituality, but to remain tuned in to the voice of the spirit within us along the route.

For Bob and me, our longing was to encounter a deeper grasp of our spirituality and we did. Not as we may have thought we would, kneeling at the steps of a cathedral soaking in the reward as we placed our offering of a 120-mile walk, but in learning that our spirituality is found in an ongoing dialogue along the way.

I came away knowing the power of a pause is found not in the number of steps we take, but in the subtle whisper calling us to stop along the way.

Pause

Part Three

Knowing It, Experiencing It, Enjoying It

Chapter 10

The limitation of our expectation

Sitting at a café overlooking St James Cathedral in Santiago de Compostela, Spain, I watched the scores of pilgrims flooding into the square. Some arrived limping, helped along by fellow travellers, whilst others looked fit and fresh. A common theme on the faces and in the expressions of their bodies was relief and fulfilment. I noticed that arriving at the foot of the cathedral steps, the long anticipated destination, were two companions in particular, and I watched as each in turn peeled the backpack off the other's shoulders. Small but noticeable indentations where the straps of the pack had cut in were evidence of a weight they no longer carried. An obvious relief could be seen in the way they straightened up and blew air out with a smile in that way we do when we put a heavy weight down. Weeks of walking now behind them, this was the moment to savor. They had arrived at their spiritual place.

It struck me that this transcendent moment was one they shared. How rare an occasion it must have been to experience the same spiritual richness in the same way at the same time.

Along with most people willing to haul a backpack for days, people with the spirit of adventure, they would no doubt take long walks again. Yet as I watched them, it occurred to me that each adventurous journey we take in life is unique. The two pilgrims I watched that day hung close to each other and looked intently into one another's eyes. From where I stood it seemed something – not words, for they did not speak – was passing between them. For a long minute, a slow trickle of tears tracked down their weathered cheeks. This was followed by a touching embrace, which I perceived to be a deeply shared sense of intimacy. At that specific moment, the moment they embraced each other, they were not marathon runners reaching a personal best or individual overcomers of an endurance challenge but fellow travellers in life who had encountered a shared moment of profound spirituality at the end of a long anticipated journey.

They were people of faith whose spiritual eyes had been opened in a way that required no discussion or need of articulation, just a shared acceptance that a door had opened to the spirit within them. They found themselves at the end of a pilgrim path discovering that what they had hoped for, even expected to find there, was an encounter as much with the life of their own spirit as that of their God.

From a 1,000-mile pilgrim walk to a sixty-minute religious service, we invest time and effort expecting to encounter our God or connect with the spirit that is within us. The two women on the steps of the cathedral I saw that day had achieved a great deal in miles and memories, but I sensed they found what their expectation could not quite voice – a deeply shared spiritual moment. What part does our spiritual expectation or anticipation play in the journeys we take? After all, are we not seeking or searching with a goal or experience in mind?

My grandson looked intently into a troubled and dramatic sky one late August and pointed to a rainbow. "Do you think there really is a pot of gold at the end of it, Granddad?" We seem to be wired to want to find something, to follow, to search or journey with an outcome in mind. Gold prospectors walk miles in the heat of an Australian outback waving their metal detectors like a magic wand. They are always in hope of that million-dollar nugget, which if found will drive them on to seek out the two-million-dollar nugget.

Whether we search for gold in a colorful sky or across barren land, a discovery that stops at a physical find may fall short of what we truly hoped the gold would bring. If asked what he would do with the gold at the end of a rainbow, my grandson would talk about fast cars and football, childish ideas of happiness. So the gold is the start not the end of the search, and one that will no doubt fail to deliver. This is the same in the search for a deeper spirituality. We dig into ancient texts, sit at the feet of a guru, or meditate on the imponderables, yet profound enlightenment comes in those moments when we least seek it. Spirituality often arrives disguised in unexpected clothes. Like digging for gold, we sense it is there somewhere yet the shovel comes up empty – most of the time.

I have met many people of faith who reach towards their God with a spiritual desire that is often tempered with a sense that their desire is not what delivers a spiritual return. On the occasions when a spiritual encounter does occur we are sometimes surprised to discover that the connection forged is with the spirit within us as much as with the God we seek. This connection is one that we cannot create but one we seem to stumble over whilst seeking spirituality.

We knock on doors knowing that, as Jesus said, one will be opened. To pause is to find a door that surprisingly opens just as we are moving to knock at the next. It is as though our expectation of an answer becomes more familiar with the doors that remain closed rather than those which open. At the entrance of a profound spiritual moment, the encounter we cannot explain, we realize it was not our knock that opened the door but the hand on the other side. Such is the stark reality that we cannot take control of the spiritual realm by means of our mental and physical efforts: however hard we knock, however far we walk or long we pray, we will always be surprised by the flood of spiritual air that comes when discovering a moment of pause.

I have come to recognize that housed within this searching is often a vision of an ending which fulfils our expectation. Maybe you can identify with what it feels like at the driving test center when the examiner turns and says, "You have passed." Or a midwife declares, "It's a girl." These moments are thought of and imagined in advance and along the journey towards the driving center or delivery room. Depending on what kind of character we are, our expected outcome may be kept close to the heart or broadcast from the lips. We might be one of those people who enjoy talking it all out. A confident extrovert might say that when she gets to the test center, she expects to pass – that's what she went there to do. She tells everyone as a way of building confidence and securing her vision. Others may internalize and appear quiet, but underneath they too will have strong images of what they hope or expect to happen. Those two pilgrims earlier will have imagined the moment of arriving in the cathedral square before arriving, and in their own way they will have constructed an expectation. We all do this.

Sharing his story of a deeply spiritual encounter, a friend used the phrase, "I wasn't expecting it, and I don't know why it happened to me." What happened is that he encountered his God in a profound and life-changing way. At the time of his encounter he was most likely emotionally and mentally stirred, but he also described an otherworldliness which I took to be his spirit within him connecting with his God. I did have my doubts, but not about the reality of the encounter – rather about the fact he *didn't expect it*. I question what he did expect from sitting in a church service praying to his God and reading off his bucket list of spiritual hopes. Was he any different from the two women walking hundreds of miles towards a site of religious significance, praying as they went? What my friend should more accurately have said is, "I wasn't expecting *that*." He was at least expecting *something* even if it were silence. Maybe this is the point, that expectation has a role to play in our spiritual encounters but does not determine or define the encounter.

I have no doubt that many people walk pilgrim routes for recreation and have no spiritual expectation. This is just like churches, temples, and synagogues having visitors who are there out of curiosity or familial tradition. Yet even these people, in a quiet moment of reflection, will be looking for more than exercise or the comfort of following what mother did. That said, perhaps you are one of those people, as I am, who are searching and seeking out a deeper spirituality as we journey in life. Ours is a journey with expectation. Because of this there is no small measure of frustration when our hoped-for spiritual encounter doesn't materialize. Yet we press on, and knock on the doors, not out of curiosity or religious obedience; rather, we do so from a desire to yet encounter that which only the spirit within us can know.

So it is possible that our searching will meet with a sense of anticlimax as our prayers of petition or feet touch the last step of a pilgrim path, only to find an emotional or intellectual rather than a spiritual experience. It is perhaps more common than not to find our spiritual expectations unfulfilled by our efforts to create them. Is it, I wonder, because we have over-prescribed to an imagined encounter or drifted into drawing spirituality with an emotional brush or our intellectual pencil?

In the past decade I have completed a number of coast-to-coast cycle rides, mostly with friends. When we hit the sea, which marks the end of the ride, some of us excitedly articulate the feelings and thoughts we have. Sometimes we philosophize, and at other times we declare our intention to do it again. Yet, every time I return from a ride, it is with scribbled notes about the experience and even an outline idea for a book. (It's a great book as all unwritten books are!) Some people say they arrive at such significant places and see them as an ending, about which they held little or no expectation. I confess that on a number of occasions, though tired and looking forward to my own bed, I do feel better and fitter than when I set off. Yet I do also look for some profound enlightenment – and the lack of it can be an anticlimax.

One of the wisdom books, Ecclesiastes, holds this helpful sentence out for our consideration: "The end of a matter is better than its beginning..." The end here is not better for the end's sake but better because it opens up to the next and possibly richer promise. How often have we heard someone say, when receiving a gift, that it is better than they could ever have expected or imagined? I think that once we imagine something we move to the design phase and neatly attach some clear expectation to a thing. This is how we think, and in the cerebral functional world we are right to exercise this process. But very rarely is this helpful in the realm of our spirituality because it removes the joy of the unexpected. Of the Christ, one writer said that he "is able to do immeasurably more than all we ask or imagine..." It does not say don't ask or imagine, but don't be limited by your asking and imagination. To specify what we expect spiritually by way of an encounter with our God or with our own spirit within is to limit our openness to what we could not possibly imagine.

My use of the pilgrimage story in this chapter is illustrative of the way we step out of ordinary life to pursue an expectation in the same way we may by attending a place of worship or working through a book during lunch breaks. We are, perhaps very subtly, looking to buy into if not own outright a deeper spirituality. The feeling of a completed pilgrimage will be good if we simply expect to complete a journey. We will have gained no more than we expected or imagined. Yet there is something more profound which is not purchased by the execution of our expectations but by accepting they are limiting on a spiritual level.

Somewhere just at the edge of the apparent end of a matter is a door to a place where we might put a breath into the sentences of our lives – a place where we are stripped of all questions and where more than we can imagine takes place.

Maybe the steps of the cathedral, pot of gold, or spiritual books studied are better when not seen as the destination but rather a point on the compass we are passing, a growth in our knowledge. Our expected destination is to discover a richer spirituality. Along our pathway of seeking greater spiritual encounters as we move from point A to point B there will be many opportunities to "Come to the end of a matter," to loosen our grip on our defined expectations. Looking through the lens of the camera, the photographer will say, "Hold it right there." Before she captures the frame, we hear the words, "Don't move – pause." Yet all day the photographer has snapped away when no posing was taking place. The couple, weeks earlier, gave a list of images they were expecting from the wedding day, but now they have to let those expectations go, lest they miss out on the pictures that will be most talked about, the unplanned surprise moments. There are moments like this in the spiritual realm too.

A spiritual pause or peek through the door to where our spirituality is most at home is not necessarily something we can usher in on demand, but what we welcome as an unexpected gift in the midst of our expectant hearts. We might be able to increase the possibilities by not seeing the steps of the cathedral as the goal of our expectation – as the end of the matter. Rather we recognize that it is at the release of our expected outcome that our spiritual eyes may see the space where our physical being will not go. The experience of many, including myself, is that these moments are indescribable, yet greatly desired, and often brief, almost over before they begin.

Such moments flow in and flow out, confirming deep in our inner life the mystery of what we might describe as points of divine connection.

Searching with expectation feels on the surface like a personal and individual pursuit, yet we are not alone in this quest. If not actually walking side by side, it is often the case that our intentional seeking of spirituality takes place in the same space as others. The sight of spiritual or religious gatherings tells us that people want to search and share in a community that is seeking spirituality.

The sceptic may well take the view that those gathered are merely filling their minds with dogma or finding friendship in their loneliness. One associate said to me that joining a bowling club or political party can furnish us with what we need. Yet I beg to differ. Many of the people we find inside a church, temple, mosque, or synagogue are sharing in something beyond the body and mind. They are in some way joining their individual search for spirituality with that of others.

There is of course a great deal of intellectual and emotional energy at religious gatherings, yet in many people there is more – an inner desire for something which we humans instinctively know to be of the spirit. It is as though we sense, if not outright recognize, a synergy with our individual and collective desire to experience the spirit within us. We are all somewhere on the continuum towards a deeper spirituality. By standing together, we help each other get beyond the limited wisdom our intellect has stored. It is as though we have a very individual spiritual need which can in some way be met by gathering together. Could it be that we are stimulated as much by the seeking of another as we are by our own search?

Working as I did for many years with programs to help those less well-off, I have long held that everyone who presented for help was genuine. This drew me into many a long discussion about the people that slipped through the vetting net. People would say, "What about that man who used his money for drugs and asked for a food parcel because he couldn't afford to eat?" In my mind he had a genuine need which happened to precede the need we were addressing with food. By coming for food, he was gathering with others on the same overall pathway to a less dependent life. He was acknowledging that he was in need, that he lacked something but was not clear what it really was.

Is this not the same in our searching for greater spirituality? We attend a temple, shrine, or worship center because it brings us closer to others who are searching. I wonder what part that "getting together to explore spirituality" plays in our arrival at moments of pause?

Solomon, the ancient Jewish king, wrote, "As iron sharpens iron, so one person sharpens another." This proverb is for me a way of expressing that in sharing the journey, the seeking of a richer spirituality, we can refine our individual spiritual journey together. When I prepare our food, I love to take the knife I chop with and sharpen it with a long round sharpening steel. The sharpener has the same properties of the knife, steel, but is shaped differently. When Solomon wrote his proverb, a common sight would have been a guard sitting in the courtyard running two blades along each other, perhaps restoring the edge or sharpness lost in a battle. The intention is not for one sharpened sword but two. When you and I rub shoulders in our searching for a deeper perhaps more meaningful spirituality, we influence and stimulate the spirit within. This search is not limited to physical gatherings, although they have a significant influence, but even in the reading of books we are engaging together, sharing what it means to be a spiritual being.

Expectation forms a significant part of our journey. I wonder where we would travel without it. Yet what we do with our image of what we expect can limit what may be possible spiritually. However individual we sense our spiritual quest to be, we are not alone in this pursuit. We seem to find ourselves drawn to others who ask and seek and knock. Should a door to a moment of pause or an entrance to a profound spiritual encounter open, it might be that we share this encounter not intellectually or emotionally but at the level of the spirit within us.

Pause

Chapter 11

Spiritual intimacy between us

When my wife and I are out for a meal and get to dessert, we can go one of two ways. If there is enough room left, we have a dessert each, mostly the same dessert – apple crumble and custard. Her crumble, sitting in its own bowl, looks the same as mine, but I guard mine in case she sneaks a spoonful when I'm not looking. On other occasions when we come to dessert and neither of us could eat a whole one, we share by ordering one dessert and two spoons. On the surface it may seem the same, just apple crumble in one bowl instead of two but the experience is much more intimate. We are not observing or identifying with what the other is eating, we are actually sharing the very same experience.

In the previous chapter I spoke of two women in Spain on the steps of the cathedral in Santiago. The image of those two women embracing at the close of their Camino stirred my curious mind with the question, "How deep was the spiritual connection they forged that day?" I have often wondered if those two women I saw were actually having a common moment with the spirit within rather than simply recognizing it in each other.

Until now I have spoken of a moment of pause very much as a personal individual experience, a deep connection with our interior – the spirit within us. Now I want to explore the question of whether it is possible that in our searching for spirituality two or more people can find that their connection is not simply with the spirit within them but a spirit-to-spirit encounter. I'm not talking here of a cerebral agreement or a conjoining of spiritual aspiration but an intimate communion, a moment in which the spirit within one person is engaged with that in another.

It was in 2018 when I was sitting outside a café overlooking Santiago Cathedral's square when I watched those two women work their way to the cathedral entrance. They no doubt went on to do what my wife and I had done just an hour earlier. Once inside the cathedral, Cheryl and I had joined the long queue of devotees winding up the narrow steps behind the giant statue of St. James. We, like the thousands before us, touched the worn and shiny shoulders of St. James, then kissed his head. It is at his shoulders where many pilgrims find their journey's fulfilment.

Earlier that day when those two women disappeared through the cathedral doors, I had wondered if they had found their journey's fulfilment in a moment of shared intimate spiritual experience and not at the shoulders of the great saint.

Is it even possible that the spirit which is in one person can encounter and experience the spirit which is in another? How would we identify this taking place? When we think of the closeness with which we can share our bodies with another and how aligned our thoughts can become, should we at least be open to the possibility of spiritually intimate moments?

As a Christian I have come to recognize with ease the concept of God's Spirit being active in a way which the spirit within me can identify, and yet the very hint that this same level of intimacy can happen human to human is a challenging thought.

We all have a spirit within us which is unique and special. This spirit was present at birth and some would argue existed before we were born. The poet William Wordsworth expressed this idea when he wrote, "Our birth is but a sleep and a forgetting: The Soul that rises with us, our life's Star, Hath had elsewhere its setting, And cometh from afar." The image here is one of the soul/spirit having an origin, existence, and future not bound by the body we clothe it in and the mind we contemplate it through. I like the idea that the spirit within me somehow predates me but brings no memory of that time. My own view is that this life is one of creating memories or personality which will be retained by my spirit as it continues the return journey to my God.

Wordsworth saw what the writer of Ecclesiastes understood when he penned, "And the dust returns to the ground it came from, and the spirit returns to God who gave it." To think of our spirituality is to think of an element of our being which is as independent as the big toe is from any complex thought that passes through our mind. Our constant challenge on our journey towards a deeper spirituality is to discern when and in which ways the body, mind, and spirit are operating.

Few of us doubt that the body and mind experience the world in different ways depending on our contact with others. Social isolation has been used for millennia to control and harm people. When society imprisons a person, they do so principally to take away their liberty to interact with others at will. I recall visiting a prison when I was training for ministry. Many of the men I saw were hardened criminals with some element of violence on their record sheet. Yet tears, often shed, were brought on by loneliness and separation from the people they loved. The realization that they could not hold their children or kiss their partner or visit a sick mother was a powerful reality to them. At times I observed that violence was a warped way of having much needed physical contact with other humans. This is similar to sexual activity in prison, a form of human intimacy craved for and not simply explained by lust.

To forcefully place a person in solitary confinement is to take them as close to the death penalty as possible. No matter how much the guard may say, "It's only until..." the one locked up has no influence over their own life. In my brief experience in prison chaplaincy, I heard many inmates speak of the despair of loneliness and dark thoughts of hopelessness solitary confinement brought. Thoughts of death or self-harm are common in these situations. Society, perhaps without consciously recognizing it, can move people labelled criminal away from the human contact that in part makes us human. Social isolation is a kind of death to a part of our being, part of our humanity, the emotional and physical part that enjoys others' company.

It follows then that direct contact with other people brings to us life in the fuller dimensions so missing in the deprivation of incarceration.

Sure, some of us may enjoy being alone, yet even the most introverted of us will desire life at some level of human interaction. We take this for granted. By and large, most of us go through our days unaware of the affirmative role touch and feel plays.

During the 2020-2022 pandemic, people were told not to hug, shake hands, or breathe too close to others. Masks hid facial expressions, and conversations took place through windows. Sadly, many people died with no physical contact or even sight of the person they most wanted to hold them. Interestingly, during the pandemic when high profile government ministers or national health advisers were caught having affairs, the reaction was not outrage on moral grounds but for breaking social distancing rules.

Society is now more aware than ever that a child sitting in the bedroom staring at a screen is not having the kind of human interaction needed to prepare them for a rounded life. Running around kicking a ball, climbing trees, and dancing – playing with others – are how we are stimulated physically, emotionally, and yes, spiritually. When our bodies are stimulated by being close to each other, an intimacy can take place which brings us into human alignment, a common experience. We are eating out of the same bowl as it were.

During my years working in the busy office of a not-for-profit, I was known for bursting out in spontaneous song. There must be very few sentences we can utter that are not part of a line in a song. A name is all it took some days to set me off

– and occasionally set me on a collision course for trouble! In our office we had that lady named Caroline. I remember once bursting into, "Sweet Caroline, good times never seemed so good..." My singing was not as good as Neil Diamond, but it was received with good humor. I found that these shared relaxed moments often brought us all closer together; we had a feeling of being united in something. There is an intimacy to be found which reveals what I would describe as a mental and/or physical connection. We simply feel or think in a way that blurs or even removes the things that separate us.

Having found someone we love and who loves us, we set off on a journey. As time goes by and joys and troubles come and go, two people may arrive at a deep sense of being inseparable – *as one*, the ancient Jewish scriptures describe it. There is a level of intimacy which seems to remove our sense of individuality, a point when we lose ourselves in another and they in us. Between life partners, the obvious place this finds expression is the sexual act. We might hear people describing the depth of their love for another person, saying, "I can't imagine life without her..." "He is my world..." It is not uncommon to encounter the story of an elderly man or woman losing all desire to live after the loss of their life partner. The phrases, "My better half," "My other half," "My soul mate," are all used to signify that two people have arrived at a place of seemingly indivisible unity.

It seems to me that on many levels we humans need connections which blend us together. I enjoy a good discussion and have friends who find pleasure in taking the opposite side of a proposition to the one they actually agree with. Yet there is something satisfying, even beautiful, when two or more people arrive at a point of agreement – to become one in thought.

For a few short years when I was younger, I worked fitting windows, something we did in teams. One day I was at the top of a ladder passing a tool to my friend Mark who stood on the inside of the opening where the window would eventually be fitted. He commented that we had not talked or pointed at a tool, screw, or any other piece of needed equipment throughout that day. He and I instinctively knew what the other needed next as we worked together. Mark said that we were becoming like an old married couple!

So we can and do discover moments of shared physical and mental intimacy – moments when we sense we are not eating from separate bowls but sharing the very same dessert. It is hard to deny that we humans have a capacity to become incredibly close, intimate, and hold a common experience, at least on a physical and mental level.

Exploring togetherness in his book *Reaching Out*, Henri Nouwen reflects on a number of areas in which people encounter shared experience with and of one another. In one such encounter with a friend, Nouwen comes to realize that they have recognized the presence of God in each other. His friend said, "It is the Christ in you, who recognizes the Christ in me." He goes on to say that he came to see that the "togetherness of friends and lovers can become moments in which we can enter into a common solitude." To pick up on this idea of solitude for a moment, I want to say I do not see this as merely an experience of being physically alone or in emotional isolation. When we seek spirituality through solitude, we are not primarily aiming to be alone but to be very present with ourselves. Those who practice spiritual disciplines which involve solitude are not merely looking for a quiet corner to be alone in. They seek a state of being which is uninterrupted by others in the physical world. This makes it even more interesting that Nouwen saw the possibility of a common moment of solitude.

We have little problem recognizing that our minds are capable of deeply intimate agreement, acting in an almost synchronized way. This is also true of our physicality in the way our bodies can find moments of what feels like timeless even thoughtless intimacy. Many communities hold all possession in common – owned by all and owned by no one particular person. They might say something is ours which includes them but never mine. This leads me once again to ask the question: Is it possible that the spirit within us can coalesce around a moment in common spirituality, a moment not described as mine but ours?

It is an important point to distinguish between a oneness which says we are all really the same thing and a oneness in which individuals are experiencing a unity of experience. Whilst Nouwen talks of identifying with the Christ in another, a Hindu reading the Upanishads might speak of identifying with the Atman. Atman is a word used in Hinduism to describe the Universal Self which makes the spirit within me, as I describe it, simply part of a whole which will one day be absorbed into what is known as the Greater Self. Other religions have similar views which are reaching beyond the ego, the conscious and contemplative self to a oneness with the life force or God. Ultimately this view is not of a unique and individual spirit within each one of us but of a spirit which is part of a Universal Self. I believe that the spirit within us is more than a *chip off the eternal spirit*, soon to be returned with no name attached. I am convinced that we are individuals with a spirit within that is unique and will return, as we read earlier, to God, but with the marks of our personality. I accept that this is an abstract thought and one based on the idea that life beyond our return to the dust is one in which we are consciously aware of who we are.

Along with many commentators throughout history, I would say solitude is a word used to describe a state of being which is more akin to the spirit within us than the world around us. You and I can enter a place of spiritual solitude whilst sharing the same park bench because it is not about where or with whom the body is sitting. I have said in this book that the realm of the spirit is not subject to, nor necessarily communicates through, our intellect or feelings; we simply use our words to interpret or translate what we experience in our spirituality. Spirituality is more than a sensory reality even though we articulate our spirit encounters through language often descriptive of emotions, feelings, or intellect.

That we cannot *think* our way into the spiritual realm does not mean that the spirit within us has no point of communication or acknowledgement with the spirit within another. I wonder if those moments we know not to be emotional yet have a deep sense of intimacy are moments of common spirituality, even a common pause. Anne Morrow Lindbergh writes in her, *Gift from the Sea*, about an intimacy of individuals coming together for a brief moment: "Making one world between them. There are no others in the perfect unity of that instant, no other people or things or interests."[20] She goes on to say that it is a moment, "Free of ties and claims, unburdened by responsibilities, by worry about future or debts to the past."

I suspect these moments of spiritual unity or common pause are broken quickly by the harshness of our mind's desire to contain or control or communicate what is happening. Lindbergh says, "And then how swiftly, how inevitably the perfect unity is invaded: the relationship changes; it becomes complicated, encumbered by its contact with the world." Yet, however brief these encounters are or remote from what we understand from an intellectual perspective, I strongly suspect my spirit to be of the same ilk as yours and so capable of intimate encounter. Right here and now in an intellectual way we are sharing this journey of exploring what it means to be spiritual. We are considering entry points to the realm of the spirit within us and maybe for some what it means to encounter God who is known by spiritual means. We are using the language and imagery of the mind to poke around and point towards a better mental understanding of our spirituality, so I ask, is it not reasonable to recognize that the spirit within us has a way of transacting which only God and the spirit in another can know?

Personal encounters of spiritual restoration are something many of us can recognize and relate to. A profound sense of the presence of God or otherworldliness are typically thought of as individual moments, albeit that they can happen in concert with others. Yet as my own spiritual journey continues to unfold, I am more persuaded than ever that there are points in our lives where two or more people can enter the space in-between. No doubt the two women I saw at the cathedral had deeply individual perspectives, yet they might well have been experiencing a shared spiritual connection, a moment of common pause.

Many of us have little difficulty in seeing our spirituality as something that happens between us and our God. That connection seems obvious. What seems less obvious to consider is a person to person spiritual experience and may require a new way of thinking about spirituality. So I leave the question for you to ponder – is it possible that the spirit within one person can connect with that in another?

Pause

Chapter 12

Fording a river and finding a fighter

Growing up in a home with three sisters, I often craved a brother. When cornered in the playground by the school bullies, I would romance about the way my big brother would step in to offer protection. There were other occasions when I would imagine the reverse. Myself as the elder brother strong and tall, the hero and go-to in troubling times, we would have had an inseparable bond. I guess we all need someone to protect us.

Over the years I replaced the older brother with texts or helpful lines from books. In fact – confession time – I talk to the odd text here and there, even an imaginary chat with the author. It was 5:41pm on May 15, 2017, whilst waiting for a connection in Atlanta Airport, when I struck up an imaginary conversation with Malcolm Gladwell over a particular line in his book *David and Goliath*: "Men, money and matériel aren't always the deciding factor in a battle." For the remainder of my journey home I pushed those words around and tried to figure out what help they could be in the coming months.

Arriving back at my office, I typed those words and stuck them on my door. As each challenge crossed the threshold, I tried not to be influenced by the position of a person, the depth of their wallet, or the size of their organization. It's one of the things I do – copy out a line or two that I like and put them everywhere. Some lines remain current in my thoughts for weeks and some will remain for a lifetime! For a season during my time as CEO at a not-for-profit organization as each December loomed, I would mine the books of the Bible and other writings to locate a line to hang the coming year's spiritual thoughts on.

In the months to follow I would be looking at each word, say in the Gladwell sentence, for wisdom and direction as I moved forward with decision making. Some of the serious decisions arriving in my lap of responsibility were made better by the presence of these words in my thinking. You see, this was not for me an exercise in academic study or the gathering of theological theories to enhance my understanding. Responsibility can be burdensome and I found this burden for me mitigated as I considered my chosen phrase or lines – an exercise which often drew me to spiritual contemplation.

The sometimes fear-laden path of what may or may not happen tomorrow – I find is smoothed by my chosen lines and helps towards letting go of, as one hymn writer says, "The cares of this world."

So one year on Christmas Eve I typed, printed, laminated, and hung the words, "I won't let you go until you bless me." These were words spoken to God by Jacob, the younger brother of Esau, during a wrestling match not going his way. If ever he needed an elder brother to step in, this was it. Esau was Jacob's older twin so there wasn't much age separation – a matter of seconds. We might think, "What's a few seconds matter?" Well, who arrived first in this context is like asking, "What's the difference between first and second in an Olympic race?" You will always know who crossed the line first; they're the one holding the gold medal and first in line to appear on your cereal packet!

In terms of Esau and Jacob, inheritance or birthright came to the one born first, which put Jacob at a disadvantage. To make matters worse, Esau was big and strong, a kind of old-fashioned man's man, hunter and fighter which Daddy Isaac responded to. Jacob, on the other hand, seems to have enjoyed hanging around the camp, a softer, sedentary stay-at-home kind of chap. These brothers broke friendship for twenty years.

Their reunion was a massive event. It was preceded by Jacob reaching out to his brother to meet up. When Esau heads towards Jacob with four hundred fighting men, it doesn't look like a reconciliation party is on his mind!

Out of fear that Esau was on the attack, Jacob parks his whole family and worldly goods in two groups on one side of the Jordan River, thinking that at least one group will escape. He then gets his feet wet crossing a ford with the intention of spending the night on the opposite bank alone.

In many ways, Jacob stands at the door of a pause where he will discover the naked reality of his own existence. The story tells us it was here that he made a significant spiritual, even divine, connection.

This is where the story gets transcendent. Before the two brothers could be reunited Jacob had to stand between all he had been and what he may become. Standing in solitude, a mysterious man appears and wrestles with him till daybreak. Most scholars identify this *man* as God, and I have no reason to dispute them.

This biblical encounter with what might be at the outer edge of mortality has for centuries intrigued those of us seeking spiritual enlightenment. Fortunate to have looked in many people's Bibles over the years I often noticed the words, "I won't let you go unless you bless me," from Genesis 32:26, had been underscored and even doused in a yellow highlight pen. These are words that many people hold on to and I found myself drinking deeply into my soul.

Is it possible that on occasion we recognize the presence of what is God and know not to let go easily?

Throughout the following year, I read and reread this story in a way that is similar to what is called Ignatian Contemplation – reading with your imagination. Ignatius of Loyola taught that we can access a richer and more personal experience of the scriptures through this route of using our imagination. At first this idea didn't sit well with me because my background churchmanship had been more focused on taking a clinical approach to interpreting ancient scriptural writings. There are those who would find it uncomfortable to stray beyond the accepted interpretation of a verse or story, believing that using our imagination leaves us open to flights of fancy and even error when it comes to important teachings. They might find the use of imagination to be flawed as a way of understanding matters of faith but I see it as an extra tool.

I was able to reconcile concerns around accurate use of scriptural texts on the ground that my use of Ignatian Contemplation, or more to the point, my own imagination, is just that – mine. In my journey of spiritual development I have been seeking to identify and stimulate a connection with the spirit within me. I have not sought to create a theological conclusion based on an ancient text. There is mystery about our spirituality and a degree of individuality in the way that we come to understand ourselves, our spirit, and even our God.

So part of my journey involves Ignatian Contemplation. In this we bathe in the story and drift in the wake of each character's experience. We learn not so much to read but to enter the story. We walk with Jacob by the river, feeling the breeze and experiencing that same moment or situation. Our eyes become accustomed to the shadows as darkness falls. For me this meant getting in touch with a sense of solitude as I contemplated Jacob's aloneness. The image is not of a lost child on a beach drowning in a sea of unfamiliar people. In reading the story, I sense there is in Jacob, surprisingly, less panic and more pondering.

I'm sure there was an element of what we might describe as panic in Jacob. After all, in the morning he would meet his estranged brother with his 400 fighting men. It would give some rise to anxiousness if not outright fear in most of us. In life we encounter such situations seemingly so momentous that we feel sick to the core, unable to sleep, eat or focus. Countless times over my years in leadership an upcoming conversation twisted in my gut, though I have never had 400 soldiers at my door! Yet in tense situations, prayer, fasting, and even wise counsel sought from a close friend could only scratch at the surface of my fear. Yet as I returned time after time to Jacob standing alone on the riverbank, I learned that it is okay to let go of this world and my fears for a while, to find a place in-between as it were of what has been and what is to come.

Jacob must have stood watching the light flicker on the water and the image of all his possessions on the other side fading in this moment whilst something greater took hold of him. It doesn't matter if the wrestling started at nine in the evening or two in the morning. What's important is that he was first alone and then on the threshold of change. As the morning dawned and the wrestler, aka God, wants to leave, Jacob holds on for dear life. I wonder if the strength of his grip was not in the muscles of his arms but his sense that the wrestler may well unlock the next step in the unfolding of his life. I suspect that even if he wanted to, Jacob couldn't unfurl his fingers. Such was his grip that we might imagine him as a rock climber knowing the safety rope had gone and his life depended on digging those fingers in.

Our concern here is not the outcome of the blessing. We are thinking about the moment alone, the space between having left his all on the opposite bank. It is nice to think the brothers' reunion went well because Jacob wrestled and refused to give in – but life is much more complex than that. The wrestling match left Jacob impaired. We must never forget this man woke every morning with a limp and struggled up every step. We don't know if his nights were restless and the pain intense till the day he died. What we know is that this was a pivotal point in his life. And we know we all have them, moments when we know things will change.

With each painful encounter in life, whether with God or a friend, the possibility of walking away limping exists. Yet sometimes a limp disguises a blessing impossible to have had without the wrestling. I share these thoughts not to focus on the limp, the pain, or the terrible scars we can receive, but to note the sense of being alive that being alone and wrestling with God can bring. Of course we can never be truly alone, for as Ignatius of Loyola said, "God is in everything." Yet we can find moments, in-between spaces, where we might experience the forming in us of a deep, divine connection.

There are times in life when facing a major transition point that it is helpful to share a kind and encouraging word, even a poem to bring some perspective to a friend. Yet there is something more profound – enriching – solid in our moving beyond shared words or even the presence of another. There are times when the space where we find a moment of pause is away from the center of our friends and counsel and possessions. There are things in life, as the Jacob story demonstrates, which are better faced in solitude away from all our other reference points in life. I'm not advocating morbid introspection or sulking in a corner but the great benefit of finding some space to be in solitude as Jacob did on the riverbank.

As we encounter situations in life which we know are major transition points, some perhaps with unclear and potentially harmful outcomes, we might do well to uncouple from all around us. Like Jacob, we must seek out places where all the noise in life becomes silent.

One of the things I like to do is listen to the last note in a piece of music played on a piano. As the key is struck the sound is clear, even crisp, but quickly, like a bungee rope reaching its end, it begins to recoil. With my eyes closed I listen to that note from the piano with my ears straining to follow it back to where it came from. I am of course following the echo of the sound, a decreasing echo back towards the silence from where it came. When I arrive there, I have blocked everything out, all other sounds and I discover a deep stillness.

Jacob seems to have travelled along the echo of his pain and fear as though it were a sound he traced back to a place of silence and solitude where he found a rich and deep audience with his God.

Those words, "I won't let you go unless you bless me," remind me to follow the echo back to the riverbank and the fire and the wrestling. However much we feel alone and would dearly love to have an elder brother or sister come and stand by our side, it is only by being alone that we truly discover the spirit within us and our God. In some ways I suspect that being alone is a pause from being part of the describable measurable definable world. To be alone and perhaps wrestle with God is to find a place where we discover our soul secured to a deep unprovable certainty. It is to be reminded that we are more than the material that surrounds us, the money in our pockets, and even the people we love.

Of course the morning comes as it did for Jacob, and the difficult conversation or decision still happens. You still have to face whatever or whoever it is. Yes, it's raw and real. We will have times when a measure of regret and failure fills our cup, when we have to sit in a soup of our own human frailty and pain. None of us are immune from the "If only I had done..." syndrome. So why bother leaving all our possessions on one side of the river and stand on the other side alone when there are decisions to be made and situations to face?

I suspect, as I have experienced in life, following a night of pause on the riverbank, we never return in the morning quite the same. Standing with me in the morning and in the difficult circumstance has been an elder brother far superior to the earthly one I had craved in my mind as a child. Few of us experience this night of wrestling followed by a morning of "I won't let you go unless you bless me." But to learn how to follow the echo beyond the sound is to move beyond our own unfolding story and our reasoning with the substance of what we see.

I often read this story of Jacob wondering if his riverbank pause, the experience of full contact with his God, lasted the whole night or the last few seconds of his grip. When did he realize that he had actually encountered God? He wanted something to take back with him, something that would help sustain him beyond the river. Not an army or erudite phrase to disarm his brother but whatever his God would give.

The practice for me of choosing a phrase each year was not a memory verse held like a talisman or incantation to influence an external outcome. At the close of each year and to help negotiate the challenges in the next twelve months of carrying responsibility, I found great depths of resource as I left all to one side of the river and forded to a place of solitude. There and alone it was often those chosen words which opened for me a moment of pause, the return was always with blessing.

There are so few things which truly demand an immediate response. Fire, flood, and famine do not call for pondering verses or weekend retreats, yet most other life events and challenges can wait whilst we dwell by the river and wrestle by moonlight. There is something powerful about leaving our possessions and our importance to one side of the river whilst we dwell on the other side alone and vulnerable. Not a vulnerability of weakness or resignation to what will be will be, but a deep openness to the spirit within us and to our God.

Pause

Chapter 13

Only just accessible but worth the reach

It was a summer weekend when my parents visited us at our home in North Yorkshire. At the time, we were attending St Andrew's Bible College, digging with spiritual shovels into our understanding of what it meant to be a person of faith. Having moved from Coventry, a busy noisy industrial city of half a million people, we were now living in a small town no bigger than the housing estate I grew up on. It was a welcome if somewhat dramatic change. For a few months, we missed the crime and craziness until we bedded in. Amongst the highlights was the odd loose cow or sheep escaping the local livestock market. It was this rural aspect, scarce amenities, and the lack of home's hustle and bustle which appeared to unnerve Dad and Mum. We get so accustomed to the noise around us, that silence becomes challenging.

Looking for something to do with our visitors, I noticed on the map an area around Robin Hood's Bay that we had not yet explored. There was a path, the Cleveland Way, along what appeared to be a rugged and promisingly beautiful part of the coast. The name of our destination was Hayburn Wyke, Wyke being one letter short of our family name – Wykes. It occurred to me that it would be really cool to have a picture of us all there, to create a memory and talking point for family gatherings. Knowing my parents would not naturally be described as outdoor pursuit enthusiasts or dedicated ramblers, I got us by car as close as possible. Our destination was the secluded bay at Hayburn Wyke with parking a little over a mile from our photo opportunity.

To my mind, a romantic at heart, I think of a secluded bay always as sheltered, warm and oozing with a sense of the exotic.

Those that can anchor their boat in such places are there to enjoy the solitude of a beautiful beach, one void no doubt of others. Yet most of us don't have a boat, and so the seclusion and solitude is less accessible.

How often have we experienced that the inaccessible or difficult places to find can bring us unexpected moments of pause. It may sound counter to what I have said elsewhere, yet I suspect the entrance to a place of pause where we might encounter a deepening of our spirituality is not a place easily reached. Have you ever turned back on a walk or a drive wondering if only you had gone on another mile? Let me share two things that helped us to recognize the invitation to pause and to encounter touching base with the spirit within us and our God in a secluded place.

On the day in question and in the absence of a boat, we needed to walk. The route took in a part of the Cleveland Way with its well-documented and stunning coastal views. I remember the look on Dad's face when we parked at the end of Salt Pans Road, a narrow, unmaintained, grass-growing-down-the-center-strip of tarmacadam. "Call this a road?" Dad shouted across to us as we clambered from the car.

It all went downhill from there! The pathway steeply dropped away, followed by what my dad thought was a goat track. Unused to such terrain, Mum and Dad humored us for twenty minutes. There I was, trying to create a memory of us being in a beautiful bay with a wild sea foaming the rocks, yet to my parents it was an unnecessary scramble along an uneven path. "I have a better idea," said Dad. He suggested he would treat us all to fish and chips on Whitby harbor front. The decision made, we turned back to the car.

In a way it was hard for me to turn back because I really wanted us to all experience being down in that bay together. The truth is we can't always share the same desire or drive, we can't always move together at the same pace. It seems that the path to some destinations, however accessible to one person, may not be to another. None of us is alone in a desire for a deeper spirituality, yet our journey is from different places towards a clearer spiritual experience.

In my writing and your reading, is an exploration of our own desire to better understand the journey to moments of pause. I have been plotting out the routes which have taken me closer to what often seems inaccessible yet deeply rewarding. Over time I have found that by reading what others have said, and reflecting on our own spiritual journey, we can better voice the prompts which lead to encounters with the spirit within us.

Many times I have encountered enthusiastic people in the throes of a spiritual experience which has enlivened or touched them at a profound level. As they enthuse about their newfound spiritual excitement, I may have a lack of interest or struggle to share their joy. To them this is like unrequited love, a one-way street of emotion, excitement, or shared discovery. I share this because it is a challenge at times to remember that we are a community of seekers after a deeper spirituality, but we don't all travel at the same pace. We might have to hold back on our excitement in a discovery or desire whilst others adjust. I knew my mum and dad would have loved the sights and sounds of that bay, but no matter how much I enthused, they were not ready for the experience. We sometimes turn back or tone down a little for the rest of the community.

Later that year Cheryl and I returned to the path and found our way to Hayburn Wyke where the views were stunning. There was even a small waterfall to take in. What we found was at the end of a path we had not travelled before. In one sense it was like a surprise gift that drew us in by the way the land had been carved to enfold this small space on the edge of the outstretched vastness of the North Sea. Descending to sea level was not easy but made more possible because we *wanted* to. Any mention of this place now reminds us of a moment of stillness at the end of a path.

For a time the words "Hayburn Wyke" entered our family folklore. To mention this place to Dad brought out his story of how we walked to nowhere and found nothing. He would laugh and talk about not listening to me when I suggest we take a short walk to find an interesting place. Dad would say, "It's not short and there's nothing interesting at the end of it." Secretly I suspect he enjoyed that day, a day when he found out his name was on the map. It was also a day when he found a useful tale to tell at his local bar, a story he told with good humor. His was a life shaped by a world that wants to see purpose or reward before setting off. Likewise, many of us see a walk's purpose as going somewhere to do something, not to walk for the sake of walking.

I have often wondered about what Dad really thought when he said, "Walking to *nowhere* to find nothing." You see, in the search for spiritual encounters which touch or move the spirit within, I find that the actual walking, for want of a better description, is *the thing*. It seems to me it is in the movement of each step we take, not necessarily the route or perceived reward, that we come closer to ourselves and to the spirit within us.

I wonder if my parents had pressed on that day not so concerned with the where to but the wonder in the walk, would they have enjoyed the moment more. Would they have found something in the journey which brought them to, if not the point on the map, then a place less material and more metaphysical in experience?

Each day and in every spiritual step forward I, with all humanity, battle with this desire to be going somewhere and discovering something, a battle born in a misunderstanding that we can't be going *nowhere* and we must be going somewhere. Can it be that there is sufficient purpose in just the journey!

Part of the reason we looked for that bay was ancestry, a look at where we came from. Many people want to know their ancestry, and a sizable industry has grown to service that interest, to scratch that itch. Such a search or itch has not come to me yet – maybe one day. That said, spotting our name on the map was a start, but not because we were hunting down a distant billionaire uncle. It was an opportunity to understand something of a possible meaning, an image if you will, of what Wyke means.

If only these things were so simple!

Much of the coastline in this area between Whitby and Robin Hood's Bay in North Yorkshire seems inaccessible either by land or sea. In many parts the land abruptly ends, falling in a steep drop to the sea, offering little or no opportunity to climb up or down. Great for those movies where everyone stands looking over the top onto the body below – no heroics as they all wait for the helicopter to arrive. Before you overthink this: no, my name doesn't mean "Dead body at the bottom of a cliff"!

It seems the word Wyke from which our name is derived can describe a place where a boat can land safely on shore and where there is a pathway to the clifftop. In short, a sheltered but accessible bay or inlet. Had we walked on a little further with Mum and Dad towards Hayburn Wyke that day, the way down to our sheltered bay would have become evident and our memory richer. Yes, it was steep and, yes, it looked hard to get to the sheltered inlet beneath, but it was not impossible or beyond us. Perhaps with better planning (and maybe if I had done a better job of selling my vision of what pressing on might bring us to), we may have made it. We may also have needed a helicopter for the return!

We might take this word "Wyke" or at least the meaning of it as a metaphor for how it might feel to seek and discover a touching place with our God. The image is of a place secluded and not found on the normal run-of-the-mill pathways. The journey to a Wyke bay is one that leads to a place of seclusion where access is often via a steep path on which few walk. It is as though you have to want to be there, that there is an inner voice whispering, "You won't know until you arrive." And you don't!

Many years ago, I spent a whole day keeping a friend away from his home whilst my wife did the same with his wife. We were a distraction, a decoy if you will, whilst their family set up a surprise anniversary party for them – or so I was led to believe. My wife and I had told them we were taking them out for a meal that evening, and so we collected them at seven o'clock and delivered them to a building which was all in darkness. As the four of us walked towards the entrance, my friend said, "I left something in the car, you go ahead." You guessed it, as I walked through the doors, expecting to join their family, the lights came up, party poppers flew and a hundred of my own friends and family shouted, "Surprise, Rob!" It was days before my fortieth birthday.

However you describe God or your brand of spiritual understanding, some of the richest moments of encounter can be found as a surprise or an unexpected gift. You won't know until you get there.

Some thirty years on from our adventure with Mum and Dad, my wife and I descended another steep cliff-like terrain in Northern Spain during a sabbatical I had been granted – my Great Pause, as I referred to it! The last fifty meters were clearly dangerous, but as we pressed on we found a rope. Kindly, some locals had staked a thick rope into the rock face which led to the beach below. Unfortunately Cheryl had not abseiled before, and although she did really well, her feet slipped, resulting in scratches, bruising, and stiffness for some days. It was all my fault! We did, however, reach the beach below, and managed to enjoy the warmth and shelter this remote place offered.

Our experience that day could not have happened were it not for the rope placed there before we arrived. We would have had to turn back, not because we wanted to, but because lack of access prevented it. Though logic and the intention of those who placed the rope there may argue it was not for us specifically, nevertheless that rope turned an inaccessible bay accessible to us.

I wonder how often we notice such aids lying in our pathway. I suspect the offer of support on the journey to places of seclusion, solitude, even spiritual encounter are not entirely by chance.

Looking at maps is pleasurable for some, myself included. It's great to see the vastness of the planet and then zoom in to see the detail of an area. The end of that rope I mentioned dipped into the sea where the Bay of Biscay and the North Atlantic meet. These vast oceans bouncing off the landmass as our feet found a sheltered but accessible inlet where these two met, a Wyke if you will.

It was here where there was seemingly nowhere else to go forward, being boat-less, that we paused. Our experience was one of feeling protection and of freedom. It seemed for a short time this place offered us sanctuary from thoughts of how to get back up the rope to the road! These are moments when we come to a natural end in the pathway, and nature or the environment appears to hold out a hand of invitation, an offer of permission, to stop and to simply *be*. This specific moment of pause for us came at the cost of some time, energy, risk and, for Cheryl, a few scratches. Yet as we paused with no particular place to go, shielded in what the powerful Atlantic had shaped by its force, the kiss of the presence of God was with us. When the spirit within us found breath, we could only describe it as a moment of utter connectedness.

Julian of Norwich was an Anchoress who lived in the 13th Century. Amongst the things she was known for was her deep sense of what pressure people lived under and their unquenched thirst and search for peace. Sheila Upjohn describes it as a: "Relentless lack of peace."[21] This is a peace we have all sought for in things – in possessions and holidays and jobs and relationships. The wise words of Julian on this matter are sobering: "Here we seek rest in things that are so little there is no rest in them." As I read Julian's words, I am reminded that to pause is not to possess some object that I perceive to help me rest or do something designed to calm me down, but to embrace my life at a spiritual level.

It is a challenge to adequately describe what a pause is because it can mean so many different things. But there is a central theme – your body, mind, and spirit neither want nor need to be anywhere else in that moment. Some will describe this as being present in the present; others use the term *connected* with reference to us all being energy or part of one big whole. My view is that of Ignatius – that God is in all things but is not those things.

Perhaps we overthink in our desire to control what is in fact beyond our control and understanding. I wonder if it is in those moments not planned, when we are not purposely contemplating or meditating on the wonders before us, that we discover that our God is reaching to us through all things. I believe that only our inner being, our spirit within, can differentiate.

There is an unexpected beauty when discovering a place of seclusion and solitude both in the physical realm and the spiritual realm. In such places our five senses can become alive, sparking all kinds of sensations. There is also, in moments of solitude and seclusion, a spiritual sense, a stimulation that can be described like a child when tickled, wanting it to stop and yet continue at the same time. The spirit within needs no outward display for this sense of utter beauty and mystery to be happening, yet it is more powerful than the activity of our five senses.

To pause is to come to the end of the voice of those five senses, allowing that other expression of our being, the spirit within, to breathe.

It is as though we enter a place of being present with the spirit within. Our spirit, this other sometimes neglected or sidelined part of what makes us whole, sees beyond to the indescribable, unmistakable sense of utter contentment in the physical realm to where some might recognize the presence of their God. I completely get why we might use the phrases – "At one with the world," or "At one with ourselves." May I offer another – "At one with our God"?

Many people say they find the notion of connection with God or even the idea of a God utterly remote, unlikely, even beyond consideration. I'm not here to argue for God. Many of us have images and experiences of quiet church buildings or temples with incense burning or rows of people bowing. For some, the rhythmic sound of the *adhan*, the Islamic call to prayer, or the ring of a church bell, ushering us to connect with our God, is a key that never quite unlocks that mystery of the kiss of God's presence.

You may have entered such places, but emerge disappointed because the encounter brought no spiritual fruit. The omnipotent supreme creator didn't show up! Personally I love historical religious environments and go to them regularly, but the kind of connection with God we found that day on the beach was unplanned, unexpected, and at the same time utterly authentic. Is it possible that we are looking, on occasions, in the wrong places?

Showing to some friends the picture I took of Cheryl abseiling that day, I was asked what caused us to press on to what was a remote maybe dangerous place. I think it was curiosity, egged on by a desire to not limit our lives to the safe and obvious. You and I don't need to dangle by a rope from a cliff to find a place of solitude and seclusion. We don't need to stand at the edge of land and sea to be enveloped in the protection of an accessible pause. Yet these images serve as a challenge to me, a reminder that sometimes to go that extra mile along the path and to trust a rope left by another may bring us to a place of being connected with the spirit within and know ultimate contentment.

It is my faith experience and expression that allows me to suggest this contentment is like the kiss of the presence of God. Whatever our religious orientation, we are seeking to reach beyond our body and mind to where life is not bound by the safe and obvious.

A pause isn't easily reached, and we shouldn't return to a particular place and expect the same moment to happen. We don't all have the same desire at the same time to pause, but sharing the journey is beautiful. I remember in the early days of building a relationship with Cheryl, I would put my face close to hers, close my eyes and lean in. Nothing in the past or the future played a role in that present moment as I waited, not rushing away, hoping for a kiss. I wonder if the discovery of the kiss of God's presence, which is the most personal intimate moment we could ever experience, happens when we pause with nowhere else to be.

Pause

Chapter 14

Wear and tear

Some years ago my sister and her husband visited Rome. On their return I listened to detailed descriptions of buildings and statues, fountains and frescos. On photographs, they pointed to various places that were familiar – Vatican Square and the famous balcony were images we all have seen from TV coverage of Easter Mass or the instalment of a new Pope. In a picture taken whilst looking towards that balcony, it is possible to see to the left a huge stone statue of St. Peter the fisherman holding a key in his left hand. In fact everywhere we look there are keys, because keys are the symbol on the Papal coat of arms. Millions believe that Jesus gave the fisherman known as St. Peter the keys to unlock the kingdom of heaven.

Most of us at some point in life will be asked to bear responsibility, to take the lead, to hold the master keys. It might not at the time seem a big thing, but the receipt of a set of keys represents responsibility for something. If the master key is in your hand, then you have become a gatekeeper.

To misplace our keys is a big deal, especially when we are about to leave the house. If I shout, "I can't find my keys," the reply from my wife is often, "I know." This exchange is usually followed by me frantically turning out drawers and digging in the settee with her casually picking them up where I left them.

One British man encapsulated the scene I just described in a song. Mr Zip, a contestant in a 2012 UK TV talent competition, sang two simple lines whilst excitedly patting his pockets and dancing from foot to foot: "Where's my keys, where's my phone – where's my keys, where's my phone..." Years on, we as a family are still singing this line as we leave the house.

It was September 1996. A master set of keys was handed to me along with responsibility for a charity's assets and future. It didn't feel like being the Pope! It *did* feel like a weight that would need more than physical effort and clever thinking to handle – I sensed a spiritual depth would be needed too. One of the keys in my care fitted the gate at the rear of the building. The building was old and the gates were made of metal and three meters tall, used for large vehicles and staff to enter and exit. The lock was round in design so as to make it hard to smash it off. A simple turn to the right to unlock and back again to lock with a small key was all it took. This process of locking and unlocking happened thirty to forty times each day.

One morning the gate lock broke, rendering the twenty-five keys dispersed to the team seemingly useless. Advice came from every quarter. Some of the team used their key to go out and get lunch. For them the broken lock was a major incident, a three-minute longer walk to use the front door! My task was simple, or so I thought – a new lock and twenty-five keys would solve the problem.

Nearby I found a small, family-owned locksmith. I'm sure you know the kind – friendly with time to spare and a dog in the corner chewing a bone. Something about that day told me that I was going to learn a lesson worth remembering.

Simon, the owner, just wanted to talk and Dave, his brother, clearly wanted to work. They reminded me of the story of Martha and Mary, two of Jesus' friends – one seems to be all commotion and the other contemplation.

Each of these characteristics holds distinct benefits. Commotion can be industrious, active, creative, serving. Whereas contemplation brings out thoughtful responses, kindness in conversation and causes less dust! The downside is that both the busy industrialist and the calm considerer can fall into thinking what they do is more important or valuable than what the other person is doing.

Whilst Dave made a commotion hitting some metal in a vise, eyeing with suspicion his chatty brother, I asked Simon for a new lock and twenty-five keys.

Simon began to dispense his in-depth knowledge of locks. It was like an episode of *CSI*. Just as I began to fade to the sound of blah blah blah, the interrogation got more intense: "Where do you use this lock, who uses it, what's the maintenance regime?"

It was this question, "What was our maintenance regime?" that sparked these thoughts before you now. I had a broken lock and a set of keys, but there was a missing third element, something that may have prevented this crisis – if a broken lock is a crisis!

Until now it was a lock on a gate, just a lock. As the words, "The drivers, warehouse staff, and a few admin folk all need their own key," left my mouth, I sensed a new interrogation coming towards me. I just knew the locksmith would ask, "Why do they all need a key!"

He did. His displeased face made me wonder if a training course was on its way! He then held the lock up so I could see it and pointed out the small dents where it had been dropped. Guilt washed over me, and, like a child with chocolate on my chin, I said, "I didn't do it!"

I began to wonder if he didn't want to sell me a lock at all. Then again maybe he was about to go in for the sting – the big bucks sale. I expected the usual sales pitch, "What you need, sir, is…" followed by words like gold-plated, super-strong, titanium.

But no. Simon was a genuine lock lover and proved to be an honest chap.

You see, walking into that shop, I was convinced by my own wisdom that we needed a new lock and keys to match. If one key had snapped or worn, a simple replacement would do, but no, the lock was done for! But Simon saw it differently. Holding the broken lock up for maximum visibility, the locksmith looked at it and said, "I can give you what you want, a new lock and keys for just over £100." Before I could respond, he said, "*Or*, I can make you a new lock to fit the keys you already have for £25, which is what you need!"

I handed over the £25. I also bought a can of lock oil with clear instructions to regularly lay the lock down resting in a little oil. *So, what's your maintenance regime?*

On the "New Lock Day" as I now call it, I made some discoveries. You and I know we don't have all the answers – which means sometimes the words of a craftsman can maybe sound boring but it's worth listening. Some stuff needs filtering of course – locksmiths love locks and so urge you to oil your locks. True, but will we? Maybe this lock thing is just a reminder that we need help to separate what we want from what we need.

We may not hold it at the surface of our thinking, but many of us have blind spots when it comes to receiving a new or different perspective. However experienced or knowledgeable we are, our views and ideas are by and large based within our experience and knowledge. We might say that our perspective is just that, *our* perspective. Of the discoveries I made that day, I include that not all blah blah blah is blah! It seems to me that our perspective is less likely to change if we are less willing to listen. Part of spiritual discipline is to listen – and to listen is to learn.

Holding the lock in my hand that day, it struck me that I had no idea what it looked like on the inside. I imagined cogs and pins, springs and sprockets but I did not know. When I think of the spirit within me I wonder if I know what is there, what shape or form the spirit within me takes. I know that a doctor can lay my body on their workbench and mentally identify each of my parts. They can say what it does and how it works. A psychologist with diagrams and some educated guesswork can explain how he thinks my brain forms thoughts and emotions.

But what of this other inner place, the spirit within me? Who can know this inner place hidden in the casing of the body and mind? A person of faith will confidently say it's their God, the great locksmith. I really do believe we too can know our own spirit within us given time and investment in seeking a connection.

Walking back from the locksmith shop, all thoughts of locks and keys were suspended to allow room for a new perspective on life. What preceded this was a set of my usual practical and technical thoughts on how we interact and where we sit in the order of life – all external stuff. At the time, my role or place in the food chain was CEO of a not-for-profit, the lock, if you will. I had a wonderful team, the keys, in this scenario. As I said, the actual lock in question was turned at least thirty times a day whereas each key was used only twice. The obvious lesson here is of course that the lock will fail first. Yet, you and I, regardless of our role in life, are at some points the overused ones, at the center – the lock, the conduit through which our children, home life, relationships, and work flows.

The lock-and-key story is a metaphor that serves to show that it's not simply a possibility that the lock – you – would be overused. It's a built-in certainty.

We can apply a million helpful techniques to control, manage, delegate, or mitigate whatever the impact to our existing in this world is. That impact can at times be pressure, at times pleasure, and the challenge we face is to create space in life for a balanced existence. Yet to seek balance in life sounds right but we often hold a two-dimensional image, say the Statue of Liberty with the scales perfectly aligned. The old saying comes to mind, "All work and no play makes Jack a dull boy." The phrase "work-life-balance" has worn a deep track in the minds of many over recent years. But I saw another path. Could the balance simply be to change how I viewed things or to change my job, become a key? No, because we will always become the lock in other situations. Before I arrived back at base with the new lock in hand I had decided it was not about work-life-balance, a poor expression of a complex reality, it was as the ancients so often taught – body, mind, and spirit balance.

There is deep refreshment for our entire being when our balance includes equality of space for our spiritual life. To pause is to give breath to the metaphorical lungs of my spirit. For five years after placing that new lock on the gate, it survived through much use and abuse. I put its survival down to us having a team member who regularly found the time in his lunch break to remove the lock and lay it on a bench with a little oil dripping through. He was purposeful, even obsessive about it.

Reflecting on this dedication shown to the preservation of a lock, I thought about my own commitment to maintaining spirituality. It would help to regularly lie down as it were and pause the comings and goings in life and give some space for the oil of silence and stillness to work through the spirit within us.

Within a year of our Lock Oiler leaving us, the lock became rusty and stiff and was, to put it mildly, done for! Yes, another trip to Simon, though I chickened out of going myself and sent someone else!

That story of those two sisters, Mary and Martha, is a reminder that constant busyness needs to be paused for contemplation, rest, refreshment. It turns out that the sister making all the noise spouted, "What I'm doing is more important than what others are doing." She was told by their friend Jesus that there are times when the lock needs oiling. In a way he was saying there are times when we need to put down the tea towel and pause.

Sometimes we feel like we are a conduit for other people to travel through – like a lock being used by multiple keys. Every time a key enters and exits a lock a small amount of wear and tear takes place. That is what happens to us as people move in and out of our lives. The reality of living in a busy world with much interaction can wear us down and sadly, for some, bring on a crisis – a broken lock! I wonder if you have known those moments in life when the constant use of the mind and the wearing down of energy has brought a breaking point or a crisis closer? Think about how obvious it is that the use of a lock without oil will result in it slowly, perhaps imperceptibly, becoming stiff then breaking.

Thomas Merton writes about the significance of our spirituality and our connection with it in terms of it sustaining us even when we may experience a measure of brokenness. Self-reliance and human grit are not what ultimately get us through the knocks of life. Merton uses the word faith to describe a deep inner sustaining resilience, a resilience which is ours regardless of our outward experience.

I see no conflict in recognizing what Merton terms faith as a connection with the spirit within us. Believing in God requires faith, and to speak of active faith is a way of describing a link from the spirit within us to the Spirit of our God. Merton writes,

Self-confidence is a precious natural gift, a sign of health. But it is not the same thing as faith. Faith is much deeper, and it must be deep enough to subsist when we are weak, when we are sick, when our self-confidence is gone, when our self-respect is gone... True faith must be able to go on even when everything else is taken away from us.[22]

What cannot be taken from us through the rigors of life is the spirit within us, yet our access to it can be overshadowed by the responsibilities that bring wear and tear.

Finding moments of pause is time not simply away from the demands made on our mental capacity and physical well-being, but time when the spirit within us is refreshed and renewed.

Pause

Chapter 15

The fine line

Easing into the seat, knowing it was all over, I felt my body relax in a way it hadn't for the last fifteen days. Sitting to my side and looking a little jaded, Eileen would, if she could, be grinning with pride at her own achievement. I grinned for her and said a little thank you under my breath. Together we had travelled 890 miles in the past fifteen days from Land's End to John O'Groats, literally the bottom to the top of Britain. Eileen is my trusted bicycle named after the woman in my life who most inspired me with cycling – Mum.

As I relaxed, feeling a little lonely, the enormity of the ride hung in the air. There was an obvious achievement in what I had done and I had gained a greater understanding about myself, new information, if you will. Yet I wondered if it were possible to penetrate beyond this stuff in my head. My fidgeting hands tidied the box which clips onto the handlebars. Maps, phone, keys, wallet, cycle glasses, and food all spilled out. In general, food fills most of the box, explaining why Phil, my cycling friend, refers to it as Rob's Nose Bag. Placing each item carefully and in order on the table before me, I lined up the removable lenses of my cycling glasses, clear, yellow, and sunshade grey.

Now on the train and in an empty carriage, I struck up a conversation with those three lenses that lay before me. I thought about how I had seen, on my ride, every hill and valley, sunrise and sunset through one of those lenses. As I looked now at them and not through them, I was filled with questions. No doubt my questions were rising from a feeling that I was at the end and the beginning of something. My body was very alive from the physical challenge of the journey and my brain busily processing the sights and sounds, people and places. In my notebook and my mind were images and stories enough to fill a thousand dreams.

I sensed a desire to move beyond my mind and body, a desire to connect with the spirit within me. Addressing my three companions, aka lenses, I asked, "How do I connect with my experience spiritually?"

I believe the activity of the mind and the activity of the spirit within are different. They are generated from different places and are distinct from each other. When we perceive something, it may at first appear that there is only a fine line between the mental and the spiritual. Yet I believe and here offer that what appears to be a fine line between the insight which comes from the spirit within us and that which is discovered through our creative and complex mind is not so fine. Both the mind and the spirit are of course necessary and valid. Yet they are different.

Over many years I began to recognize that to pause from our question-driven mind is to travel a different pathway, to see from a different perspective. I sometimes think of it as though I am lowering a bucket into a well from which I rarely draw water, making the process at this well unfamiliar. Imagine the bucket is a different shape and the rope of unfamiliar material. Lowering this bucket into this well is not the same; the tools to draw refreshing water are different.

I wondered, as you may have too, what triggers or tools could help us to move in the direction of this spiritual well from which to draw spiritual insight. When I ask how I connect with spirituality, I recognize there are specific ways to approach this, and some seem no different from mental activity. This is why that fine line between mental and spiritual may seem finer when we attempt to express the insights gathered from the spiritual area of our being. We use words, as I am here, to make familiar and logical sense of our spiritual encounters. The explanation, for instance, that I give about the spirit within or moments of pause sound like the product of my thoughts world, yet the source of the actual spiritual insight is from the spirit within. It is perhaps here where some might consider this to be hair-splitting – but it's not. What I'm suggesting and exploring with you is that there is a difference, however subtly expressed, between insights from the mind and those from the spirit within us. The challenge is that it takes us on a journey that feels unnatural or too alien to every other approach we take in life. I used to think this is easier for people of faith, but it is not.

Arriving at an obvious or natural change in direction, a fork in the road of life, in the case of my cycle ride to arrive at the most northerly point of the country, can bring us to a place ripe with desire for inspiration. For some of us this is exciting and stimulating but scary too. In the same way that a scientist may come to an impasse or artist stare at a bare canvas, so can a seeker of spiritual insight and encounter hit a wall. A path must be taken, a connection formed, but which?

The scientist will interrogate and analyze minute details as they roam through data creating and exploring different pathways. The artist may engage with feelings, emotions, mood and light. My search or questioning on the train that day was, in part, philosophical and at the same time spiritual. It was never about knowledge or feelings but a desire to connect with the spirit within me, to move beyond the mind and body. The struggle to get traction in these situations I suspect is that in our desire for spiritual insight we overanalyze the data, miles travelled, places visited, information gathered, or money raised. Or we may look more into our emotions asking how we feel. Helpful as these lines of travel may be they are not about being immersed in the spirit within.

As I have said throughout this book we are more than our mind and more than our body. There is a significant part of our being which operates aside from data processing and tingling feelings we call emotions. Yet identifying the entrance to and activity of this abstract aspect of our being is a challenge.

Is it possible that in seeking spiritual insight we can on occasion travel familiar mental pathways which lead not towards the seat of our spirituality? For the most part of our waking hours we operate from a logical mind set. This mind set seems to hold that we can work towards spiritual understanding as though we can think our way into the spiritual realm. We read technical, theological, even philosophical books in our exploration of seeking logical answers to the evidence or ideas of spirituality before us. But can we use such tools to examine or mine the realm of the spiritual?

Of course we do develop as a person through intellectual engagement with the world around us. Many of the challenges of life are met by asking questions and forming workable answers. Yet I want us to recognize that the desire we have for a deeper or richer spirituality, a connection with the spirit within us, is not accessed via our intellectual or emotional tool bag. As we accept the need to use the tools of the mind, words, to explain spiritual encounters we reconcile that the activity of the mind is not spirituality but a way of having a conversation about it. As we shall read later it was in taking a different perspective of my cycling lenses that I was able to identify a connection with spiritual insight.

There are points in our lives such as my moment on the train when we are at a junction or place of change. This is not necessarily physical, it can simply be that we come to recognize we are more than the feeling we are having or the thoughts we are thinking. However counterintuitive it may be, to pause is to stop interrogating those feelings and thoughts. I look at it like this. I have a well full of feeling from which to draw hope and fear, love and laughter. It's the same for the well of my mind. I lower the bucket and expect to pull up ideas and data. To pause is to stop lowering the bucket into those two wells and draw from the well of the spirit within us.

You and I are negotiating our way through a technological post enlightened world which at many levels is strongly influenced by a belief that insight is there for the taking. Answers are a calculation away. Let me encourage you as a traveller into the realms of spirituality. Our journey is not in ignorance of our amazingly beautiful inquisitive mind, but we seek to draw from a source which defies the logical, rational mind. In the words of Spock to Captain Kirk, "There's life there, Jim, but not as we know it." There the context was that the tools they used could not identify the substance they examined.

The artist Salvador Dalí was best known for his weird surrealism paintings. He would hold a key over a plate as he dozed in a chair. You can imagine him sitting with the blank canvas, all his feelings and emotions worn, the light in the room not helping, so he stops and waits. As he falls off to sleep, his grip relaxes and the key pings on the plate, and he tries to capture what he was thinking within a quarter of a second before. Inspiration comes to him in that memory.

Thomas Edison had a similar routine which involved power napping. He would sit upright in a chair holding a ball bearing. As it dropped, he would write the first idea that came into his head. Inspiration. (Next time you flick a switch and light appears immediately, think of that ball bearing dropping to inspire the great inventor, our lives are better for it!)

These two, the great scientist and the great artist, found inspiration at the doorway of their questions. Many have said and I agree that these men were actively utilizing their subconscious. They were, in the minds of many, still operating out of their emotional feelings or calculations present just before they dosed. They were in fact accessing the part of the brain difficult to reach at a conscious level.

I suggest that we too can access a part of our being, the spirit within us, by means of a pause from even these intriguing pathways to the subconscious. We seek connection with a part of us which is not governed by our mind but our spirituality. Spiritual insight travels the path of spiritual connection.

I remarked about there being a fine line between the mind and the realm of the spirit within because it seems to me it would be wrong to suggest this is an abrupt step. The very nature of this conversation is one of how close, despite how different, the body, mind, and spirit within are. The question of how do I connect to spirituality, the spirit within, is one we are right to ask, yet it is the *how* which is so often the stumbling block.

The very nature of spirituality is abstract – almost unseen or hidden. My wife likes to sew and she sometimes makes clothes with an invisible zip. We know it's there but we can't see it, and even when pulling it up or down the zip is only revealed as the little tag is pulled.

Connecting with the spiritual realm is a movement from the seen to the unseen. Happold in his book *The Journey Inwards* suggests this can be a choice. He points to the character of William in the Aldous Huxley novel *Island*. William, who chose to shipwreck himself on an island not easily accessed and in a reflective mood about the two worlds in his life, expresses the fine line over which he passes. He says, "Floating, floating, like a white bird on the water, floating unresisting, effortless – between the real and the imagined, between what comes to me from outside and from what wells up from deep, deep down within me – floating, unresisting, without effort, on the surface of the great flowing river of life."[23] To pause is to move not by the effort of conscious thought but with a sense of the unplanned drawing towards something that by the spirit within we instinctively know not to resist.

Back in that train carriage I settled myself down, feet on the ground, eyes closed. I parked all my questioning thoughts. At that point I breathed and paused as though you would to meditate. In a sense, I was reducing or clearing my mind of rubble, catching that moment at the bottom of an exhale before breath returns.

Several minutes passed, during which, unawares to me, others had joined the carriage and the driver had started the engine. First the whistle and then the jolt as the diesel engine took up the slackness between carriages. My neck flopped, and my attention to the surroundings returned. I had been alone, fully present, quiet and unstirred, by what was around me.

My eyes fell on those three colored lenses on the table before me. Immediately a moment of insight occurred to me. They spoke back.

Well, I jest! But I came to an insight into the tools that help us access this realm of the spirit within us. Something of a bridge across that thin line between what is of the mind and what is of the spirit within. I scribbled words which were almost illegible.

It seemed important to capture this inspiration before it left, as I feared it would with the speed of the train as it pulled out of Wick station. By stopping my questioning mind, a break in my inquiring thoughts, it was as though an unfamiliar pathway opened which led to a deeper connection with my spirituality. From where this connection landed, like the bucket reaching the unseen bottom of a well, I drew insight. Some may say it was an Edison moment of accessing the subconscious. I disagree, yet accept this is where the fine line between the mind and the spirit within I spoke of is evident.

Show me a great invention and my brain comes alive with questions. Kiss me and my body feels the touch and arouses my emotions. In those lenses I was able to capture the echo or image of the insight which welled up from my spirit that day. I saw what part silence and solitude and stillness play in my accessing of who I am as a spiritual being. Holding each individual lens I carried across that fine line mentioned earlier between our thoughts and the spirit within, came the answer to the question, "How do I connect to spiritual insight?"

The simple answer is to say we connect first with the spirit within us from where spiritual insight comes. My religious friends might ask if I have dropped God from the equation here. No I haven't. I believe the reason we find it hard to accept the words, "God spoke to me," is because we immediately think of voices in the head. My suggestion here is that when we say there are words in our head that God spoke, I believe they most likely arrived in our spirit first. Spiritual insight does not originate in our mind. It's simply where we have the conversation about it.

Imagine cycling on the road on a bright day with clear visibility. You don't need glasses to see but you do for protection against the dust as you move swiftly along.

It was just such a day when I wore the clear lenses as I passed Loch Lomond in Scotland. It was a still morning and the water looked like glass. The lack of movement helped me to remain present, not thinking about what was behind me or ahead. You know, part of connecting with our spirituality involves stillness, being in the moment. Looking at Loch Lomond through clear lenses reminded me of this. We know that stillness has a part to play in easing us towards and over that thin line between mind and spirit. Yet I believe we have to discover this as a spiritual insight, as I did that day, not simply accept it as an intellectual concept.

That same day in the afternoon I stopped to rest at the Falls of Falloch. On approach the light faded with some cloud cover and dullness descended making visibility poor. I clipped on the yellow lens, which filters out blue light and sharpens your vision. When I wear it, it helps me to block out unnecessary distractions.

I confess I felt weird and self-conscious, dressed as a bumblebee – black hat, yellow glasses, and fluorescent yellow jacket! Fortunately I was alone. I watched the water tumble over the rocks. It was a real treat to have a pause, a moment of solitude. It seems to me that the realm of the spirit within us is a most private and deep place; a part of finding connection there is helped by finding a place of solitude, almost an external mirror of our internal reality. Ivan Mann in one of his poems wrote of this internal private deep place. This place within us which we seem to reach from an external solitude to the person of faith is where they meet with their God. Mann writes of God that love, "... comes from the deepest place – that you have made for you in me."[24] Solitude ultimately is the experience of being alone with the spirit within us and for some their God.

At the start of my long bike ride it was a really hot June 1st, so hot and bright that I questioned my decision to cycle for the next 890 miles which were in front of me.

The first three days of turning those pedals was a real slog. In my armory of cycling sight protection were the dark grey sunglasses. That first part of the ride was on busy roads. I recall the sun's powerful brightness and the noise of traffic rumbling by all day. It wore me out. Around lunch time on the second day, my head was baking from the heat and the noise, so I stopped on Dartmoor.

There was too much to take in on the main road – like saying, "I couldn't think straight" – it was just like that. In the woodland shielded from the road, a powerful silence drew me to a moment I could only describe as transcendent peace. There is no doubt that silence has a part to play in connecting with our spirituality. First the external noise needs to be held away then we learn to silence the internal voice, something I found easier when the external sound is hushed. John Skinner writes in *Hear Our Silence* of the Carthusian monk's commitment to discovering an "innermost silence" which floods the mind. "Our life's task is to listen to this silence and allow it to rule our hearts,"[25] Skinner suggests.

A favorite Psalm of many is 139. When I read it, I sometimes chuckle at a couple of the lines. They read, "Where can I flee from your presence? If I go up to the heavens, you are there; if I make my bed in the depths, you are there." I chuckle because it is like this trying to find silence – wherever you go there is noise; it's just everywhere even in your own head. The psalm writer also announces that God, "Created my inmost being." This is an acknowledgement that there is an inner dimension to us, the spirit within, I believe, which can never be away from God but can draw closer through silence.

As the train neared Inverness and there my lift back home to Cheshire, I began to repack my bar box. Everything lay as it was when the train left Wick station. Back there I had posed the question, "How do I connect to spiritual insight and spirituality?" Placing each lens in the special little protective case, I held them and answered my own question. Pause and enter the silence and take no questions with you, rest in the solitude where no one seeks answers from you and remain in the stillness till inspired.

Is it an idea that we should regularly, not just at the major junctions of life, place the contents of our metaphorical bar box on the table and pause? The questions will still be there when we return but we might just have found the insight beyond the reach of our mind.

Pause

Conclusion

For many of us our taste in music is aligned to our teenage years. The songs we danced to or heard played as we entered adulthood became anthems and wisdom to our developing thoughts. I was born in the early 1960s to parents who loved popular rock and ballads, and so I grew up on a diet of wordy songs full of messages and mystery.

In her younger days Mum was a big Carpenters' fan and the lyrics of one song, "We've only just begun…" have circled my mind for decades. At the heart of the song is the lyric, "Sharing horizons that are new to us, watching the signs along the way…" As I listen to these words, I am reminded that in our journey towards a deeper spirituality there are endless new horizons, and as we meet each one there are signs to the next.

In drawing the pages of this book to a close, I am eager to make clear that this is a beginning and not an end. I have been sharing the horizons I have encountered – horizons which I hope to be new to you or at least signs to the next encounter along your way. I believe without a doubt that each of us is in pursuit of, if not in possession of, the power of a pause. To pause in the context I have been sharing is not something we capture and contain. It is not something we create but a moment of sublime inexplicable presence, to know beyond the concept of knowledge and doubt that your spirit within you is alive and at work.

The urge to share my journey and thoughts on moments of pause came in part from an interest in the lives of mystics and mysticism. Such people form a small fragment of society and are largely unknown. Mystics are people full of wisdom and grace, and in the main they live humble simple lives focused around their spirituality as the central event of living. They seem to hold in common an eccentricity which keeps them on our periphery. Throughout the ages they have been viewed as odd – outsiders and not easy to understand. Yet they stand as a reminder to us that to seek spirituality means to let go of what others think and to be willing to travel to the borders of conventionality. Writing about what we might call the destination of meditation Bede Griffiths unfolds the elements of our being by describing the body as a: "Physical organism which unites us with all the physical organisms of the universe." The Soul, the psyche with the senses, feelings, imagination, reason and will which he maintains is, "Very limited,"[26] but beyond it is the spirit. It is my reading and journey's experience that however challenging it may be to articulate spirituality, there is something beyond our psyche that can be reached. Of those who have truly encountered the spirit within, there is little room for doubt.

Of the mystics I have found no better description than the one used by F.C. Happold,

> Though he or she may not be able to describe it in words, though they may not be able logically to demonstrate its validity, to the mystic their experience is fully and absolutely valid and is surrounded with complete certainty.[27]

The realm of the spirit within us and the notion of God to the mystics and to mysticism are all about a communion or participation with their spirit and the world of spirituality. So clear and unambiguous is this other realm that they lose the need for fitting in mentally and emotionally with the general run of society. Julian of Norwich, Buddha, St. Teresa of Ávila, Thomas Merton, and others would tell us there is a realm in which we exist that has a greater impact on the material expression of us than can be viewed through feelings or described with words. This is why they were convinced that time in contemplation, prayer, and meditation was not time available for compromise.

At the outset I expressed my own identification as a practicing Christian, yet I recognize that all the great religions hold views and expressions of what it means to be a spiritual being. I believe we learn to wrestle with and reconcile that the presence of the spirit within us is beyond the sense of material and intellectual reality. Faith in a God resolves this paradox and gives meaning to the eternal nature of our spirit which as I said earlier predates and succeeds our mortal body. It is clear that attempts to know God or enter the realm of spirituality with the mind cannot be achieved, yet they can be encountered by communion, participation, and union. This is why the Hindu will seek not self-understanding but to be freed of the self and join the Universal Self. The Sufi mystic will dedicate their lives to an inward search for God, not to blend or be absorbed but to be close to their God in a nonphysical way. The early Christian Desert Mothers and Fathers I mentioned previously took serious steps to create a life which allowed for maxim spiritual practices like meditation and prayer. A pause is brought nearer by practices that place us in the realm of spirituality. We need to be intentional in our spiritual journey.

It seems to me, as I look out from 2021 towards the future, many people are not mystics and may not be seeking the label of a faith expression, yet have a curious hunger to explore the realm of spirituality. In the main we are ordinary people living out our lives with all the complexities that life in family and community entail. We may not have found a cave in Egypt, a monastery in Montana, or an ashram in Amritapuri, yet we seek a richer, deeper spiritual experience where we are. The power of a pause it seems to me is in the discovery of spirituality in the midst of living out life in and not on the edge of society.

My aim in this book has been to suggest that the very thing we crave is fundamentally within us. I am not advocating that we move to the edge of society or fully disengage with the world around us, on the contrary. I have shown that at the heart of our ordinary experiences, on holiday, in work, walking through a park, or even in the crucible of a conflict, we can know moments when our mind and body give way to the presence of the spirit within us.

Right where we are is where our deepest spiritual encounter will take place because spirituality is inextricably linked to the spirit within us. I believe it takes the slightest of adjustments to ensure we come close to encountering the spiritual realm – to pause.

Let me offer a few very simple but helpful ways we can respond to the need for moments of pause.

On my desk is an electronic food timer with a subtle beeping sound and on my phone is a meditation timer with a low gong sound. I use them very differently because one is to increase concentration and one is to return me to it. The timer on my desk I set for seven minutes at the end of which it beeps and my flow of thought when working is interrupted. If I am focused and in a creative stream, I hit the rest button with the batting reflexes of a tennis player, ending the sound and starting a new seven-minute countdown as I continue working. This is my way of avoiding getting lost in a thread of thought that's not working or maintaining momentum when it is.

The meditation timer on my phone I set for five minutes, but only when I am relaxed and breathing calmly. Throughout my day, six or seven times, I take five minutes to meditate. Occasionally when I hear the gong, I reset, and sometimes I move beyond my thoughts and breathing to a moment of pause. These are beautiful transcendent moments, yet even when they do not happen the time in quiet stillness is part of my spiritual journey. The timer is a tool or a key to maintain a familiarity with spiritual exercises. Through this practice I have built up my time in meditation and in moving beyond it. Why not try it?

Remember my friend Paul at the start of this book and how he would sit with me in silence or chat about spirituality? Well I still see him most weeks and we spur one another on. Having a specific friend who we share our spiritual enquiry with is invaluable and more so if they don't always quite agree with where you are coming from. This is not about accountability or being in a group or even finding a guru. As useful as those are I have found simply having a friend with a similar thirst for spirituality, a companion in the pilgrimage a great encouragement. Paul and I have been as the song says – sharing horizons that are new and watching the signs along the way. I wonder who you will talk about this book to and share the ideas you have developed here with.

I have avoided being over-descriptive or using phrases which suggest there is a formula or program to follow which will bring us to a fruitful spiritual experience. It seems to me the world of spiritual commentary is well catered for in that way. I once made the mistake of putting my contact details in a web page when I was looking for an insurance quote. The e-mails came flooding in, each one an assurance that no other company could give as good a deal. If we do this with spiritual enquiry we can become inundated with offers of gurus or plans to follow. Rather than offer a program or set of instructions or living guru, you may feel more comfortable in doing what I have done in finding a character from history that exemplified spirituality and study them.

Choose a mystic and read as much as you can about them. Focus on the biographical side of their lives.

Although many would not class him as a mystic I have spent many years reading and examining the life of Oswald Chambers. His life and approach to the importance of spirituality has been more inspiring to me than his words. I have done this with many others, Thomas Merton, St. Anthony, Therese of Lisieux, St. Francis, and more recently Thomas Keating – all inspiring lives who stirred me to seek silence and stillness whilst remaining engaged with the world around me. So why not put this book down and order a copy of the life of one of these people? As you get to know them as a person and immerse yourself in the life of one who really has encountered the realm of the spirit within, the inner life, you too will journey in that direction.

Where to start the journey towards moments of pause? Near where I live is a small stream and some days I sit and watch the water till like a mantra its sound carries me beyond my conscious thoughts. I suspect that within easy reaching distance is a place where you might sit in relative calm and watch water flow or a tree move to the breeze, a place where you might practice stillness and silence. Becoming familiar with a particular spot is the start of a routine. It is quite remarkable how quickly I have found I can enter my spiritual practice of allowing nature, a stream, a tree or a grass verge, to invite me to pause. I highly recommend you identify an outside space to sit and be still.

We begin to pause when we accept that we are body, mind, *and* spirit and thus invest our time with equity. We begin to pause when we enter silence through emptying our pockets of questions. We begin to pause by finding a space in which we are not disturbed, a space of solitude. We begin to pause when through encounter with the spirit within us we know stillness, when there is nowhere else to be, and past and future dissolve into the now.

Along with the spirit within you and God, I invite you to pause.

Pause

References

1. *New Seeds of Contemplation* – Thomas Merton, p. 27
2. *Crossing: Reclaiming the Landscape of Our Lives* – Mark Barrett, p. 33
3. *Breathing, I Pray* – Ivan Mann, p. 38
4. *Surprised by Hope* – Tom Wright, p. 78
5. *Etty: A Diary, 1941-43* – Etty Hillesum (found in *Dark Night Spirituality*, Peter King, p. 37)
6. *Under Our Skin* – Benjamin Watson, p. xix
7. *Finding Sanctuary* – Christopher Jamison, p. 28
8. *The Way of the Heart* – Henri J.M. Nouwen, p. 21
9. *The Way of the Heart* – Henri J.M. Nouwen, p. 21
10. *The Jesuit Guide To (Almost) Everything* – James Martin SJ, p. 175
11. *An Introduction to the Desert Fathers* – John Wortley, p. 19
12. *The Jesuit Guide To (Almost) Everything* – James Martin SJ, p. 181
13. *The Jesuit Guide To (Almost) Everything* – James Martin SJ, p. 141
14. *Mysticism: A Study and an Anthology* – F.C. Happold, p. 18
15. *The New Creation in Christ* – Bede Griffiths
16. *Dark Night of the Soul* – St. John of the Cross, p. 79
17. *The Order of Time* – Carlo Rovelli, p. 57
18. *Seeking Differently: Franciscans and Creation* – Simon Cocksedge, Samuel Double & Nicholas Alan Worssam, p. 7
19. *Franciscan Spirituality* – Brother Ramon SSF, p. 112
20. *Gift from the Sea* – Anne Morrow Lindbergh, p. 65
21. *In Search of Julian of Norwich* – Sheila Upjohn, p. 34
22. *New Seeds of Contemplation* – Thomas Merton, p. 187
23. *The Journey Inwards* – F.C. Happold, p. 110
24. *Breathing, I Pray* – Ivan Mann, p. 50

25. *Hear Our Silence: A Portrait of the Carthusians* – John Skinner, p. 37
26. *The New Creation in Christ* – Bede Griffiths, p. 33
27. *Mysticism: A Study and an Anthology* – F.C. Happold, p. 19

Pause

Bibliography

Barrett, Mark (2001) *Crossing: Reclaiming the Landscape of Our Lives*. London: Darton, Longman & Todd.

Gladwell, Malcolm (2013) *David and Goliath*. New York: Back Bay Books.

Griffiths, Bede (1992) *The New Creation in Christ*. London: Darton, Longman & Todd.

Happold, F.C. (1963) *Mysticism: A Study and an Anthology*. London: Penguin Books.

Happold, F.C. (1968) *The Journey Inwards*. London: Darton, Longman & Todd.

Jamison, Christopher (2006) *Finding Sanctuary*. London: Weidenfeld & Nicolson.

John of the Cross, St. (2003) *Dark Night of the Soul*. Trans. E. Allison Peers. New York: Dover Publications, Inc.

King, Peter (1995) *Dark Night Spirituality*. London: SPCK.

Lindbergh, Anne Morrow (1975) *Gift from the Sea*. New York: Pantheon Books.

Mann, Ivan (2005) *Breathing, I Pray*. London: Darton, Longman & Todd.

Martin, James SJ (2010) *The Jesuit Guide to (Almost) Everything*. New York: HarperOne.

Merton, Thomas (1961) *New Seeds of Contemplation*. New York: New Directions Publishing Corporation, p. 27.

Nouwen, Henri J.M. (1981) *The Way of the Heart*. London: Darton, Longman & Todd.

Ramon, Brother SSF (1994) *Franciscan Spirituality*. London: SPCK.

Rovelli, Carlo (2017) *The Order of Time*. London: Penguin Random House UK.

Skinner, John (1995) *Hear Our Silence*. London: Fount Paperbacks/ HarperCollins.

Upjohn, Sheila (1989) *In Search of Julian of Norwich*. London: Darton, Longman & Todd.

Watson, Benjamin (2015) *Under Our Skin*. Illinois: Tyndale Momentum.

Worssam, Nicholas Alan, Simon Cocksedge, Samuel Double (2021) *Seeking Differently: Franciscans and Creation*. London: Canterbury Press.

Wortley, John (2019) *An Introduction to the Desert Fathers*. Cambridge: Cambridge University Press.

Wright, Tom (2007) *Surprised by Hope*. London: SPCK.

Suggested reading list

There are many good books out there which express, explain and encourage spiritual life. In reading around the subject of spirituality I found the following books of tremendous help in spiritual understanding, spiritual practice and spiritual reflection.

A key discovery for me was that my thought world and spiritual world behave differently. Much of my own clarity on this comes from the following books.

New Seeds of Contemplation – Thomas Merton (New Directions Publishing)

The Jesuit Guide To (Almost) Everything – James Martin, SJ (HarperOne)

Mysticism: A Study and an Anthology – F.C. Happold (Penguin)

The Journey Inwards – F.C. Happold (Darton, Longman & Todd)

Immortal Diamond: The Search for Our True Self – Richard Rohr (John Wiley & Sons)

Crossing: Reclaiming the Landscape of Our Lives – Mark Barrett (Darton, Longman & Todd)

In terms of spiritual practices and rules for living the following books gave me great insight and helped to form my own rhythm and rule for spiritual encounter.

Finding Sanctuary – Abbot Christopher Jamison (W&N)

Halfway To Heaven – Robin Bruce Lockhart (Methuen London Ltd)

An Introduction to the Desert Fathers – John Wortley (Cambridge University Press)

Franciscan Spirituality – Brother Ramon SSF (SPCK)

The Surrender Experiment: My Journey into Life's Perfection – Michael A. Singer (Yellow Kite)

Breathing, I Pray – Ivan Mann (Darton, Longman & Todd)

Crossing: Reclaiming the Landscape of Our Lives – Mark Barrett (Darton, Longman & Todd)

O-BOOKS

SPIRITUALITY

O is a symbol of the world, of oneness and unity; this eye represents knowledge and insight. We publish titles on general spirituality and living a spiritual life. We aim to inform and help you on your own journey in this life.

If you have enjoyed this book, why not tell other readers by posting a review on your preferred book site?

Recent bestsellers from O-Books are:

Heart of Tantric Sex
Diana Richardson
Revealing Eastern secrets of deep love and intimacy to Western couples.
Paperback: 978-1-90381-637-0 ebook: 978-1-84694-637-0

Crystal Prescriptions
The A-Z guide to over 1,200 symptoms and their healing crystals
Judy Hall
The first in the popular series of six books, this handy little guide is packed as tight as a pill-bottle with crystal remedies for ailments.
Paperback: 978-1-90504-740-6 ebook: 978-1-84694-629-5

Take Me To Truth
Undoing the Ego
Nouk Sanchez, Tomas Vieira
The best-selling step-by-step book on shedding the Ego, using the
teachings of *A Course In Miracles*.
Paperback: 978-1-84694-050-7 ebook: 978-1-84694-654-7

The 7 Myths about Love...Actually!
The Journey from your HEAD to the HEART of your SOUL
Mike George
Smashes all the myths about LOVE.
Paperback: 978-1-84694-288-4 ebook: 978-1-84694-682-0

The Holy Spirit's Interpretation of the New Testament
A Course in Understanding and Acceptance
Regina Dawn Akers
Following on from the strength of *A Course In Miracles*, NTI
teaches us how to experience the love and oneness of God.
Paperback: 978-1-84694-085-9 ebook: 978-1-78099-083-5

The Message of A Course In Miracles
A translation of the Text in plain language
Elizabeth A. Cronkhite
A translation of *A Course In Miracles* into plain, everyday
language for anyone seeking inner peace. The companion
volume, *Practicing A Course In Miracles*, offers practical lessons
and mentoring.
Paperback: 978-1-84694-319-5 ebook: 978-1-84694-642-4

Your Simple Path
Find Happiness in every step
Ian Tucker
A guide to helping us reconnect with what is really important in our lives.
Paperback: 978-1-78279-349-6 ebook: 978-1-78279-348-9

365 Days of Wisdom
Daily Messages To Inspire You Through The Year
Dadi Janki
Daily messages which cool the mind, warm the heart and guide you along your journey.
Paperback: 978-1-84694-863-3 ebook: 978-1-84694-864-0

Body of Wisdom
Women's Spiritual Power and How it Serves
Hilary Hart
Bringing together the dreams and experiences of women across the world with today's most visionary spiritual teachers.
Paperback: 978-1-78099-696-7 ebook: 978-1-78099-695-0

Dying to Be Free
From Enforced Secrecy to Near Death to True Transformation
Hannah Robinson
After an unexpected accident and near-death experience, Hannah Robinson found herself radically transforming her life, while a remarkable new insight altered her relationship with her father, a practising Catholic priest.
Paperback: 978-1-78535-254-6 ebook: 978-1-78535-255-3

The Ecology of the Soul
A Manual of Peace, Power and Personal Growth for Real People
in the Real World
Aidan Walker
Balance your own inner Ecology of the Soul to regain your
natural state of peace, power and wellbeing.
Paperback: 978-1-78279-850-7 ebook: 978-1-78279-849-1

Not I, Not other than I
The Life and Teachings of Russel Williams
Steve Taylor, Russel Williams
The miraculous life and inspiring teachings of one of the World's
greatest living Sages.
Paperback: 978-1-78279-729-6 ebook: 978-1-78279-728-9

On the Other Side of Love
A woman's unconventional journey towards wisdom
Muriel Maufroy
When life has lost all meaning, what do you do?
Paperback: 978-1-78535-281-2 ebook: 978-1-78535-282-9

Practicing A Course In Miracles
A translation of the Workbook in plain language, with
mentor's notes
Elizabeth A. Cronkhite
The practical second and third volumes of The Plain-Language
A Course In Miracles.
Paperback: 978-1-84694-403-1 ebook: 978-1-78099-072-9

Quantum Bliss
The Quantum Mechanics of Happiness, Abundance, and Health
George S. Mentz
Quantum Bliss is the breakthrough summary of success and
spirituality secrets that customers have been waiting for.
Paperback: 978-1-78535-203-4 ebook: 978-1-78535-204-1

The Upside Down Mountain
Mags MacKean
A must-read for anyone weary of chasing success and happiness
– one woman's inspirational journey swapping the uphill slog for
the downhill slope.
Paperback: 978-1-78535-171-6 ebook: 978-1-78535-172-3

Your Personal Tuning Fork
The Endocrine System
Deborah Bates
Discover your body's health secret, the endocrine system, and
'twang' your way to sustainable health!
Paperback: 978-1-84694-503-8 ebook: 978-1-78099-697-4

Readers of ebooks can buy or view any of these bestsellers by
clicking on the live link in the title. Most titles are published
in paperback and as an ebook. Paperbacks are available in
traditional bookshops. Both print and ebook formats are
available online.
Find more titles and sign up to our readers' newsletter at
http://www.johnhuntpublishing.com/mind-body-spirit
Follow us on Facebook at https://www.facebook.com/OBooks/
and Twitter at https://twitter.com/obooks